SECRETS
from the
SOFA

SECRETS
from the
SOFA

A Psychologist's Guide to Achieving Personal Peace

By Dr. Kenneth Herman

Editor, Jeff Steinhorn

iUniverse, Inc.
New York Lincoln Shanghai

Secrets from the Sofa
A Psychologist's Guide to Achieving Personal Peace

iUniverse books may be ordered through booksellers or by contacting:

iUniverse
2021 Pine Lake Road, Suite 100
Lincoln, NE 68512
www.iuniverse.com
1-800-Authors (1-800-288-4677)

The information, ideas, and suggestions in this book are not intended as a substitute for professional advice. Before following any suggestions contained in this book, you should consult your personal physician or mental health professional. Neither the author nor the publisher shall be liable or responsible for any loss or damage allegedly arising as a consequence of your use or application of any information or suggestions in this book.

Confidentiality is imperative to the practice of clinical psychology. Therefore, all case details (though actual cases) have been modified in name and facts to protect the anonymity of my patients. Any familiarity of content to a reader is purely coincidental.

ISBN-13: 978-0-595-41432-1 (pbk)
ISBN-13: 978-0-595-85783-8 (ebk)
ISBN-10: 0-595-41432-X (pbk)
ISBN-10: 0-595-85783-3 (ebk)

Printed in the United States of America

Contents

DIRECTORY OF EXERCISES

ACKNOWLEDGMENTS

I greatly appreciate all the colleagues, family, and friends who encouraged me to write about what I did to help my patients. Their support has inspired me to tell my story. My initial psychotherapeutic orientation was based on Interpersonal Relations theory. However, over the years I found that a cognitive-behavioral approach was the most effective method of bringing about long-range change. I am deeply indebted to my colleagues who pioneered this valuable treatment modality. Dr. Aaron Beck and Dr. Albert Ellis are to be noted especially.

I thank the thousands of patients who trusted me with their deepest secrets and had the courage and determination to explore new vistas. I learned a lot from them.

I would also like to thank Stacie Jubinski for lending her secretarial and computer skills. I appreciate her contribution.

I am indeed grateful to my wife, Benita, and my colleagues Amy Pressler, Frances Christmas, and Dan Steinhorn for reading my manuscript and giving me suggestions on how to improve it.

I am deeply indebted to my daughter Debbie and my editor and son-in-law Jeff Steinhorn for organizing, editing, and helping to shape my material. Their creativity and perseverance were essential to this book becoming a reality.

To the people of the world: May each and every human being be able to know self-esteem and peace of mind. No person deserves less.

This book is dedicated to my wife Benita and our children Mike, Debbie, Joe and Rebecca. Also, to my parents Rose and Joseph Herman. Their love for me gave me the strength to be able to love.

INTRODUCTION

My compliments to you for deciding to read this book. Whether you selected it on your own or received it as a corporate gift doesn't matter. My name is Ken Herman. I am a clinical psychologist. I have been in practice for over forty-five years and have conducted over 100,000 hours of psychotherapy. I have seen people through just about every aspect of life, from the hardest times to the best of times, those going through personal challenges as well as those growing toward personal triumphs. Feelings of inadequacy, indecision or simple malaise, dissatisfaction with a small aspect of one's life, depression and anxiety, illness and loss, death and birth, overcoming guilt, marital problems, suicidal thoughts and attempts, help-lessness, hopelessness, and despair have all made their appearance in my office. It has been my greatest reward to see individuals achieve healthy lives and relation-ships, improved careers, personal successes, and, most important, peace of mind.

Throughout my career, I have derived considerable pleasure from seeing my patients grow—I have observed the numerous and varied ways in which peo-ple have succeeded in changing their lives for the better. I have witnessed the inner strength that we as humans all possess. I have been given the opportunity to observe individuals rise from the depths of despair to heights they didn't even realize existed. In fact, this is why I chose to name the book *Secrets from the Sofa*. It has been decades since the stereotypical psychoanalyst's office contained the obligatory sofa, on which the patient lay down to share his or her innermost thoughts with the goateed, note-taking therapist. However, it is still a stereotype that people relate to today. And since my intent here is to impart to you the meth-ods I've developed and used, the tips I've fine-tuned, the practices I've seen work over and over, all from the inside of my office, in a way I am sharing with you these tools, these nuggets, these *secrets*.

Contrary to what the title may seem to imply at first glance, I am certainly not sharing or publishing any confidential information about any of my patients. I do present dozens of case examples in this book since I believe it is immensely helpful for people to see what other similar people have gone through, partly to under-stand that no one is alone—no matter how bad one's problem seems, others have probably gone through the same or worse before. And I also believe it is human nature to want to compare oneself to others. By seeing that other very normal, often very successful people have issues, problems, and difficulties at times is usually immeasurably reassuring and bolstering when going through issues of one's own. The case excerpts in this book provide those comparisons and reassurances with clarity of specific points throughout the text. However, in each and every case, fictitious names and quotes are used and no information is given that could possibly lead to divulging whom the case is actually about. I have always held patient confidentiality in the highest regard, and it is certainly not compromised in this book.

Now, what can this book do for you? Perhaps you have never sought or needed help from a psychologist or other professional. Maybe you have thought about seeking a therapist but have not pursued it because of financial constraints, time restrictions, or fear of what being in psychotherapy might mean to you. Perhaps you have received professional help in the past or currently are working with someone. Whichever your situation, in choosing this book, you have acknowledged that you have the desire to become a stronger, more confident, and more balanced person. I want to share my knowledge and experience to help you achieve growth and change. As you read this book, take what is most applicable and meaningful to you and use it to effect positive change in your life.

Secrets from the Sofa can point you in the direction of a more fulfilling life. It provides you with a step-by-step guide for overcoming a wide variety of emotional and interpersonal problems. All too often, we let our problems defeat us. Faced with a vexing frustration or conflict, we may not even know how to begin to resolve it. *Secrets from the Sofa* walks you through a process that will enable you to reach your goals no matter how unhappy, uneasy, or unhealthy you feel. I have written this book to help you think more highly of yourself, to enjoy rich, rewarding relationships with loved ones, and to lead a productive life.

There is a term I use throughout this book—the *personal peace process*. I am referring to the conscious steps we all take, day after day, to get us closer to a state of happiness, serenity, peace of mind, fulfillment, contentment, harmony, and balance, or, in my words, personal peace. Each step you take forward in dealing with issues, fears, worries, and problems is a step along your own personal peace process. In Part Three, I devote a whole chapter to the "Personal Peace Plan," that is the specific goals, strategies, and tactics that you can deploy in order to help yourself grow, become more stable, strengthen your ability to handle difficulties, and, ultimately, attain your personal peace.

Unfortunately, no book can substitute for a good psychotherapist. Depending on the nature of your problems, you may need support in addition to this book. The last chapter provides you with information concerning how to know if you need to work with a professional, and provides additional resources that may prove useful as well.

What you will learn in *Secrets from the Sofa* is how to develop a plan to address your current difficulties. Perhaps you feel lonely, depressed, or isolated. Perhaps you feel trapped in a bad marriage or a dead-end job. In *Secrets from the Sofa* you will also find actual inspiring case studies that demonstrate how others have tackled similar challenges. As you follow the steps, you will also begin to master coping skills that will improve your ability to handle new stresses as they come up. As long as you make a commitment to change, you can overcome even long-standing problems.

Since I first began practicing psychotherapy nearly a half century ago, the field has undergone major changes. After World War II, psychoanalysis was in its heyday, and intensive long-term treatment was not uncommon. Today, because of the factors like the advent of managed care and the widespread availability of psychotropic drugs like Prozac, the general time spent in therapy has been limited dramatically. Short-term therapy (one to twenty sessions) has become the norm. Not surprisingly, the editor of the bible of psychotherapy research, *The Handbook of Psychotherapy and Behavioral Change*, recently decided to eliminate the chapter of brief therapy in the last edition because, in his words, "… almost all therapy is brief now."

Secrets from the Sofa is based on the principles of the most widespread form of therapy, the cognitive behavioral approach. Cognitive is another word for thought. Cognitive therapy assumes that an individual's thoughts, perceptions, and attitudes significantly affect his or her feelings. Depressed people, for example, are often paralyzed by self-critical thoughts. Cognitive therapy attempts to bring about a change in mood by encouraging people to think more positively about themselves. Although this concept may seem simplistic, it can have a far-reaching impact on a person's self-concept, attitude, and emotional well-being.

Self-deprecating thinking can produce a never-ending cycle of distress. Cognitive behavioral therapy teaches you how to reverse this course. Once you start reaffirming your self-worth, you can begin to mobilize your strengths and cope with your problems more effectively.

Distorted thinking underlies many problems besides depression. This book will help you examine your thinking style so that it doesn't continue to sidetrack you. Unhappiness or emotional issues often stem from negative thinking and negative perceptions about yourself. That negativity is, in turn, often rooted in childhood misfortunes. *Secrets from the Sofa* provides exercises that will help you understand how your background may have contributed to negative perceptions about yourself and your future. (Many times people don't even realize they have these perceptions.) Once you make the connection between your past and your current difficulties, you can start developing healthier ways of thinking and acting. Although the process may involve some bumps along the way, it does not take forever. This book is goal-oriented and will guide you as you struggle to break bad habits and negative patterns.

However, I must warn you that change requires dedication and hard work. Patients who have made the most progress made a commitment to persevere for "the long haul." Unfortunately, for you to grow, you will have to learn to tolerate difficult feelings from time to time, such as anger, anxiety, and sadness. But if you consider that your future and your emotional well-being are at stake, the trade-off is well worth it.

Through the ages, people have struggled to find the key to personal peace. Having devoted my life to studying human behavior, I am convinced happiness cannot be purchased in a store or derived from the acquisition of worldly possessions. The most enduring sense of satisfaction ultimately comes from seeing yourself as a worthwhile person and respecting what you think and do.

In my role as a psychologist, I often observe that my patients have strengths of which they are not aware. Do you readily see yours? In the final analysis, you can count on yourself like no other person in this world. But you will never know how much you can achieve until you have tapped into your own inner resources. If you don't take charge of your life, it can easily take charge of you in the guise of unwanted habits and psychological symptoms, such as depression and anxiety. In order to reach your potential, you will need to confront issues and problems head-on. As you gain confidence, normal everyday problems will no longer overwhelm you.

Most importantly, keep an open mind. It is possible—just possible—that you are a much stronger person than you think. Give yourself a chance—help yourself. You are worth it!

Dr. Kenneth Herman

www.secretsfromthesofa.com

PART ONE

UNDERSTANDING WHY

Chapter One

WHY PEOPLE ARE NOT HAPPY

Many people travel through life waiting for the world to be exciting. Some are waiting for the ideal mate, some are looking for a more challenging and rewarding career, and some are waiting to inherit a fortune. Often what these people already possess goes unrecognized and unacknowledged. They are saying such things to the world as, "When I get older, I'm going to read all the books I didn't have a chance to read before" or, "When I retire, I will travel to the places I have always wanted to see." The problem is, most people with these thoughts never realize their "future," and what's worse, cannot enjoy their "present," often due to how their "past" has conditioned them.

The poet Sara Teasdale was, by most standards, a very talented writer. Yet she was an unhappy person who was unable to internalize her strengths. In her later years, she became aware of having passed the prime of her life without realizing that her existence had some meaning. It was too late to go back and capture all she had let slip by. Feeling that she had nothing to look forward to, she finally committed suicide.

What a tragedy it would be to reach a point in life where we must admit to ourselves, "Strange to have crossed the crest and not to know." To possess life's treasures and not be able to enjoy them is truly a waste. To realize one day that it is too late is indeed a depressing thought. I do not subscribe to the philosophy that it is too late to regroup and resolve a problem. We can't recapture lost time, but we can seek more meaningful and rewarding goals at any stage in life.

What do you feel is slipping by in your life? What brambles are catching your clothes and preventing you from reaching for a higher crest? Are you frustrated that you haven't met the right companion? Are you confronted with a weight or drinking problem? Are you stuck in a dead-end job, an unhappy marriage or relationship, or faced with some undesirable habits that you have been trying to kick for years? By now, you may have given up hope of things ever being different.

But they can be different! Once you understand the source of your difficulties and what you can do about them, you can begin to make the necessary changes.

Many of us go through life on automatic pilot. We rarely examine why we behave the way we do. We just plow ahead the only way we know how. For some, this approach works. Finding a suitable mate and building an exciting career come naturally to some lucky people, but, unfortunately, only relatively few. For many, however, being on automatic pilot leads to falling short of their potential. Rather than seizing the controls and taking charge of our lives, we settle for mediocrity because it is easy and convenient. While it may work well for flying airplanes, automatic pilot rarely works for living your life.

Childhood Counts

Over the last few decades, mental health professionals have discovered some startling facts about human development. In contrast to most other species, human beings are dependent on their parents for a relatively long period of time. During childhood, we have no choice but to trust our parents to attend to our physical, emotional, and economic needs.

Since no parent is perfect, it is not always easy for parents to meet all of the needs of their children. Fortunately, most parents do a pretty decent job. But many, too many, significantly miss the mark. There is a direct relationship between the stability of the parent and his or her ability to rear children who are emotionally secure. Less stable parents who are overprotective, for example, rob their children of independent thinking, leaving them helpless and needy. Other insecure parents who reject and abuse their children bring about insecurity, low self-esteem, and distrust in their offspring. On the other hand, parents who employ sound judgment tend to be able to raise relatively stable children.

Children need affection, discipline, guidance, limits, and loving relationships with their parents in order to grow into self-reliant, self-disciplined, and secure adults. To what extent were your emotional needs met in your childhood? Would you raise your children exactly the way you were raised?

As adults, we all are programmed to behave just as we behaved as children. If we are secure, we will gravitate toward people and experiences that promote the same sense of well-being that we enjoyed in childhood. Unfortunately, if we are insecure, we are compelled to seek out time and time again an environment that frustrates us just as our parents once did. Over seventy-five years ago, the founder of psychoanalysis, Sigmund Freud, M.D., identified this self-defeating pattern of behavior as the *repetition compulsion*. Trapped in our painful pasts, we become addicted to the familiar misery that we know intimately. On some level, we have adopted an attitude of resignation about life. After a while, we prefer not to think even about new possibilities for our future. We accept inevitable situations (e.g. a lousy job or a bad relationship) that don't really satisfy us.

Even in loving families, interactions between children and parents stray from the ideal. Despite their good intentions, many parents may unwittingly burden their children with feelings of insecurity. At times, nearly all children receive messages from their parents that make them feel inadequate. For example, parents often err by attacking a child personally for doing something wrong, rather than criticizing the specific behavior. Shouting at a child, "You are bad for hitting your sister!" produces much more shame than simply telling him or her to stop. In all families, periodic conflicts arise that end up leaving children needlessly wounded—even if just a little. Child-rearing presents an enormous challenge. Many parents, although they do the best they can, simply are unaware of how their behavior affects their children. In addition, some people grow up in families where they experience parental loss or rejection (due to death, illness, or divorce), if not outright abuse. *We can never change what happened to us in the past. However, we can change how our past affects us today.* Whatever has been learned can be unlearned. No matter what childhood tragedy or subtle negative messages we have experienced, we need not give up our dreams.

Lynn's story illustrates how patterns established in childhood can interfere with our ability to enjoy life as adults. In therapy, she developed the courage to change. She followed the very exercises presented in this book at her own pace and one step at a time. By the time she terminated therapy, she had begun to move ahead in her life, following her own personal peace process (detailed in chapter seven). As she and I would speak every several months thereafter, I would see her reaching closer and closer to her personal peace. In fact, today, Lynn would say that she is as comfortable, content, hopeful, vivacious, and balanced as anyone she knows. Not bad for someone who spent a good portion of her life unhappy, uncomfortable, and insecure.

> A successful model at twenty-eight, Lynn was referred to me by her physician. I was not surprised when Lynn initially expressed gratitude toward her parents for raising her as they did. "My mother knows best and I appreciate everything she does for me. I may not like everything she does for me, but I would never hurt her. After all, I wouldn't be so successful if she hadn't done so much for me."

Adults who have endured conflictual relationships with their parents often use denial as a defense mechanism. This stance allows us to avoid acknowledging the depth of frustration and anger that we have stored up. Denial often involves both minimizing the stress of critical relationships and our feelings in general.

> When I asked Lynn if she ever got angry, she replied, "Not often. Oh, if I am looking for something in a store, and they don't have my size, I might get a little frustrated."
>
> In the weeks that followed, Lynn began to identify and express her feelings. She discovered some important truths about herself. "You may not believe this, but until I came here, nobody ever asked me my opinion about anything. My mom decided who my agent should be, and what my schedule should be. My life is strange. I'm nervous, angry, childish, fearful, and I don't stand up for myself. It is gradually becoming clear to me. I am mixed up, and I don't know what to do about it."

Lynn was discovering her problem. She was telling herself that she had issues to overcome, and she was uncovering the source of those issues. At the same time, she was dedicating herself to improving her life. She could no longer deny that something was wrong. This first step requires considerable courage because it involves entering uncharted territory.

> Lynn was an only child. Her parents, Robert and Mary, had been married for twelve years when she was born. Her mother tended to exercise control in family decisions. Robert, who earned his living as a plumber, described his wife as "a tough cookie," who tended to be stubborn. Disliking conflict, he reluctantly agreed to let her take full responsibility for raising Lynn. He regretted not being more involved in her life during her childhood and their lack of closeness.
>
> As Lynn remembered more about her childhood, she identified how much her mother tried to control her behavior over the years: "My mother always overprotected me. She fed me long after I was able to eat by myself. Sometimes, she would insist on remaking my bed after I had made it. To this day she still asks me if I have to go to the bathroom whenever we leave the house!"
>
> Even in her late twenties, Lynn was still being treated like a helpless child by her mother. She felt as if she needed to remain a child in order to please her mother. In fact, she confessed to me her enormous anxiety whenever she even thought about taking more responsibility for her own life. By insisting that Lynn depend on her, her

mother had ended up intensifying Lynn's feelings of helplessness, inadequacy, and anger.

Lynn now realized that she had a choice. If she continued to play the role of a child, she could avoid feeling anxious in the short-term. However, this role doomed her to remaining unhealthy forever, both physically as well as mentally. She realized that she wanted more from life than just a successful career.

"Many people say that I am attractive, but on the inside I feel like a nothing person. My mother will keep emphasizing all that I have accomplished. Despite my success as a model, I don't have any self-confidence. I feel like I never grew up. I want to start acting like a grown-up."

Lynn began to set some goals for herself. She saw the need to establish healthier boundaries between herself and her mother. Eventually she was able to verbalize her realizations:

"I have been allowing the way my mother treats me to affect my life. I can't be responsible for someone else's behavior. If I don't agree with my mother and she chooses not to speak to me for a while, that's her problem."

Lynn also decided that she wanted to date more. Unfortunately, her conflicted relationship with her mother also interfered with her social life. "Every time I show interest in a guy, my mother says I can't burn the candle at both ends."

Lynn now began to take action. Armed with the insights into how and why she remained unhappy in her life, she desired to establish her own identity. She restructured her relationship with her mother. She distanced herself from her— both physically and emotionally. She moved from the suburbs to the city. With regard to her career, she slowly took charge, first, by conducting her own correspondence and later, by negotiating some of her own business contracts. She also sought out new experiences: she took some graduate courses and joined a theater group. Over time, the nature of her interactions with her mother changed. She no longer revealed as much about herself to her mother, and they started to relate to each other as adults. Those committed to change are usually able to find improved methods of coping as shown in Lynn's case.

Self Reflection Question

Can you think of any parental interactions (from your childhood or adulthood) that may be keeping you unhappy and/or unhealthy?

Childhood Can Be Traumatic

I have seen few parents who intentionally want to harm their children. Yet, unwittingly, many parents fail to meet the emotional needs of their offspring. Some parents fail because they have unresolved personal difficulties that prevent them from giving to their children in the way that is needed. Others fail through their own insecurity, fostering insecure children. Others may have impaired judgment because of a drinking problem or other substance abuses.

Bad parenting is sometimes taken to the extreme. We know that thousands of cases of child abuse are reported to government agencies, and even more cases go unreported for a variety of reasons. We know too that child protective agencies are continuously busy with large case loads. We also are aware of the fact that many parents do not provide proper supervision and care of their children, leading to young people being unnecessarily injured, engaging in improper behavior, using drugs, and committing crimes.

By citing these grim facts, I do not mean to suggest that all or even most Americans undergo severe trauma or neglect during childhood. However, childhood is much rougher than we used to think. Because childhood forms the base on which we build the rest of our lives, most adults with traumatic histories tend to be unhappy or unhealthy in one way or another.

Even under the most ideal household situations with two well-meaning, well-adjusted parents, raising children is a complex task. No parent is perfect. Problems in childhood into adulthood often stem from one's interaction with his or her parents. And often the key to self-understanding lies in examining this parent-child relationship. I say that not to find fault with everyone's parents, but rather to call attention to the origin of a lot of personal problems. Low self-esteem, for example, is practically always learned somewhere in a person's upbringing.

Self Reflection Question

Were there any issues, parental distractions, or even abuses or traumatic events that you endured in childhood/adolescence that you feel may have a hand in contributing to your current frame of mind?

Chapter Two

PARENTAL TAPES

The first section of this book discusses the long-term effects that parents' messages have on their children. These messages can be positive, and can help children develop into strong, secure, confident adults, or they can be negative, often resulting in unsettled, insecure, unhappy adults. Thinking back to my own upbringing and parents, I will always feel fortunate and grateful that my parents were supportive and loving. I certainly did not know it growing up, but I now can appreciate the long-term impact my parents' words and lessons have had on my life. In fact, some of these words and lessons from my father are actually responsible for saving my life. This example goes back to World War II, while I was serving with the U.S. Third Army at the Nuremburg trials in Germany following the war.

I was sitting at my desk when a war prisoner was brought in. I turned to look at this man who was about to enter prison for the next twenty-five years and found myself repeating my father's words, from months earlier. While I had been preparing to go overseas, my dad had cautioned me, "Don't ever take your eyes off of anyone over there—don't let your guard down for one minute, or you may never come back alive."

As I stared at the prisoner, I could hear my dad's words clearly. Although I didn't anticipate any real danger—after all, I had a Colt .45 pistol at my side—I asked the guards if anyone had searched the prisoner. Nobody knew for sure, so I got up and started searching the man myself. Inside his leather jacket was a Colt .45 similar to mine, with a bullet in the chamber and the gun set to fire.

I often wonder if I'd be alive today if I hadn't recalled my father's warning. If I had looked away, even for a moment, I may never have had the chance to live this beautiful life. Each day I wake up, I thank my father silently, not only for his words of warning, but for his years of teaching, coaching, and caring for me as a young inquisitive boy, so that as a young, invincible-feeling soldier, I trusted him and knew to heed his warning.

Unfortunately, there is a considerable segment of the American population that is carrying around wounds from childhood that have never healed. Tragically, the negative experiences of childhood never leave us. If we grew up in a troubled family, receiving specific negative messages about our self-worth, or if we grew up in an intact family, never receiving support or encouragement, self-condemning thoughts may always remain in the back of our minds. We may forget exactly what particular events contributed to them, but the pain does not go away.

I have identified five core effects that constitute ways in which we store this unprocessed childhood pain: guilt, negative thinking, poor self-concept, lack of initiative, and anger/depression. These core effects—sometimes two or more in combination—are what keep people unhappy and unhealthy. Unless identified and addressed, they may hang on to us forever, like chains that can impede our every movement.

1.) GUILT

Guilt refers to the feeling that one has behaved badly and is to face dire consequences. I often tell people that guilt is a worthless emotion. Guilty feelings often are a result of poor self-esteem and low confidence, rather than having actually done something bad.

Peggy is always feeling guilty for having done the wrong thing. When she gives her daughter a gift, she is sure that she has selected something inappropriate. She also questions what she says, fearful that she has said something others might find offensive. In therapy, Peggy identified the source of her guilty feelings. As a child, she attended a strict religious school where "kids got hit with a ruler for misbehaving." The youngest child of parents who were well on in years, Peggy also never had anyone to turn to for support. "I spent my whole childhood being the good girl." For Peggy, change involved linking her guilty feelings to these unfortunate circumstances and understanding that she no longer had "to be quiet as a mouse in order to avoid being hit." She realized that she was not that vulnerable child anymore.

Self Reflection Questions

Can you identify current feelings of guilt in yourself? If so, try to trace back over your life, when and how these feelings developed?

2.) NEGATIVE THINKING

In the 1960s and '70s, Aaron Beck, M.D., developed a new form of psychotherapy called *cognitive therapy*. The basic premise of cognitive therapy is that negative thoughts and attitudes affect our moods. In Beck's view, negative thinking—involving distortions such as exaggerating, personalizing, and catastrophizing—causes depression. Still popular today, cognitive therapy attempts to make people feel better by helping them change their thought patterns.

I often apply the principles of cognitive therapy in my psychotherapeutic work with patients. Identifying negative programming that we have received from parents or other authority figures is central to change. As a matter of fact, most people repeatedly replay the negative *parental tapes* inside their heads. Negative parental tapes are the hurtful comments we hear in our minds that our parents told us time and time again. Often as adults, we don't realize that it was our parents, teachers, or siblings that actually were the ones to say those shaming or punishing things to us. As adults, we assert that we really believe these thoughts about ourselves, and that they originated with us, but generally they come from childhood authority figures. Not surprisingly, if our parents consistently criticized us or threatened us, our negative parental tapes can take the form of harsh and negative thoughts about our behaviors and ourselves.

> John, who grew up in a strict Irish Catholic family, and was subjected to unreasonable rules, tended to personalize and catastrophize. Whenever he played a poor round of golf, he called himself stupid. He attacked himself personally, rather than addressing the problem in his inability to chip or putt on that particular day. Likewise, he catastrophized, often coming up with doomsday scenarios when he thought about the future. After spending years working toward his C.P.A., he decided that he simply could not practice. "What if I don't know what to do and mess up a client's tax return? That could be disastrous," he told me. He preferred to work in a country store.

Therapy involved uncovering how and why John's confidence and self-concept were so low. John started to realize that neither of his parents ever offered him much encouragement or support. He also remembered some particularly frightening times, namely, his first day of camp when he was ten.

> After introducing John, his mother told his counselor, "If he doesn't behave, you can do anything you want to him. You have my permission!"

It was no wonder that John always felt a sense of dread, as if danger were lurking just around the corner! After spending a few months in therapy, John summoned up the courage to work as an accountant. Eventually, he became successful, performing his professional responsibilities with confidence.

In the final analysis, our negative thoughts have a source. They don't just come out of the blue; they are there for a reason. They constitute the residue of a series of painful events in our childhood. Much of our early conditioning depends on how our parents or other authority figures interacted with us. Unfortunately, we cannot get rid of negative thoughts easily because they often have been operating for many years. But as independent adults, we no longer are beholden to negative messages that we received decades ago. As adults, we can sort out the positive and negative legacies from our childhoods and regain control over our lives. As adults, it is inappropriate to think and act as we did when we were children.

Self Reflection Questions

Make a list of your own negative parental tapes. If you can't recall what things parents, teachers, or authority figures said to you as a child and adolescent, write down all of the negative things you say to yourself currently. What are those statements that make you feel bad about yourself? It is very likely these are the forgotten comments that were made to you as a child.

3.) POOR SELF-CONCEPT

Negative parental tapes also may lead to a poor self-concept. Self-concept refers to how we feel about who we are. Do you perceive yourself to be a strong, worthwhile person? Do you feel comfortable or uncomfortable with your identity? Many highly successful people who have amassed considerable wealth and power exhibit a poor self-concept. Likewise, some people who have achieved little in the way of worldly accomplishments feel good about themselves. Self-concept boils down to what we feel on the *inside*, not what we do or have on the *outside*.

Parental tapes often include specific negative messages about our self-worth. Some people may throw themselves into their careers, seeking success at any cost in order to combat feelings of inferiority. This approach is not a real solution because such behavior still lets our past control us. If we let our negative parental tapes dictate what we do, we are not using mature coping skills. Even more important, achievement alone can never permanently change a weak self-concept.

Alternatively, some people end up agreeing with the negative parental tapes and deciding that their parents were right. They become convinced that they will never amount to anything, no matter how hard they try. Rather than fulfilling their potential, they remain unfulfilled forever.

> Peter's low self-concept led him to be an underachiever. His position in the family business did not really challenge him. He felt ambivalent about his job, and expressed some of this hostility by procrastinating and reporting late for work a few days a week. Peter could trace his lack of self-confidence to things his father had said to him over the years. His father was extremely critical. Peter told me, "When I was a kid, Dad always said I didn't have a head for school. It made me feel like I could never be a good student. I also felt guilty for asking him to pay for college. Whenever I did work around the house, it was never good enough. I didn't get the wrench right or the board straight. I knew I was going to get yelled at. He used to say, 'You're not going to make it in this world unless you shape up.'"
>
> As an adult, Peter still feared his father and avoided him. Even though he was no longer in his father's "firing range," the damage had been done. His poor self-concept affected all aspects of his life. Besides his problems on the job, Peter suffered from restlessness and boredom along with frequent bouts of depression and hopelessness. In addition, although rather handsome, he rarely dated, convinced that all women would find him unattractive.

Change for Peter meant tapping into his many strengths, such as his considerable intelligence. Improvement proceeded slowly because Peter had difficulty trying new things due to an overwhelming fear of failure.

Self-Reflection Questions

How is your self-concept? How would you rate yourself on a ten-point scale if ten points represented "highly confident?" What messages do you send to yourself? Are they mostly positive statements or negative ones? If you don't know what your self-concept is, describe yourself in one or two paragraphs. That should give you a good idea of your opinion.

4.) LACK OF INITIATIVE

As noted, the *core effects* often appear side-by-side. Peter's difficult childhood, namely, his strained relationship with his father, led to all five: guilt, negative thinking, poor self-esteem, lack of initiative, and depression.

People with childhood histories like Peter's often lack a sense of self-efficacy—the feeling that they can shape their own lives. They cling to the false belief that they are still living in the world of their disapproving parents. Assuming that all attempts at achievement will be found wanting, they give up trying.

The ability to set goals, develop a plan to meet them, and follow through comes more easily to people who have enjoyed a nurturing environment in childhood. They have internalized a caring, soothing inner voice that keeps them going during periods of frustration and stress. They understand that anything worthwhile entails hard work and patience. In contrast, adults who grew up in chaotic or uncaring families tend to be poorly organized and lack self-discipline. They may also have trouble delaying gratification. If they do initiate a plan of action, they often bail out at the first sign of trouble.

> Tom, who grew up under circumstances quite different from Peter's, also lacked initiative. A recent graduate of a small college, Tom neglected his studies and did not perform well academically. Without any specific goals or vocational aspirations, Tom took what he referred to as "the easy route" after college, and began working for his father in the automobile industry. Saddled with a short attention span, Tom claimed to aspire to succeed in business and marriage, but faced gloomy prospects unless he could make a commitment to change.

Over the last few decades, through TV and the print media, we all have heard about how much children need "role models." Unfortunately, this national dialogue tends to focus on the characters of a few famous athletes and obscures the real issue. Children need not only celebrities to look up to, but also real adults in their lives—ideally, their parents. A loving parent can both model responsible behavior and show children that they are valuable by investing time and energy in those relationships.

> Tom never learned self-discipline because he had not been exposed to it. After coming into a large inheritance, Tom's parents sought out a life of luxury. They joined an exclusive country club, and became active on the social circuit. Overlooking Tom's real needs for

attention and support, they attempted to express love by giving him money and buying him things.

Not surprisingly, Tom lacked initiative in large part because he never had to work for anything. For Tom, change would have to involve mourning the superficial nature of his ties to his parents and exploring a whole new way of living.

How often have you seen parents overindulge children with things that were not appreciated? We have an appreciation for what we work for.

Self-Reflection Question

In what ways, if any, do you lack initiative?

5.) ANGER/DEPRESSION

In response to a childhood filled with disappointment and losses, people may adopt one of two related coping styles. As adults, they misdirect their frustration toward others or misdirect it toward themselves. People in the first category are consumed by anger; those in the second by depression.

Anger is a healthy emotion. If someone violates our boundaries or threatens to take advantage of us, anger can mobilize us to protect ourselves. For adults who have endured a tempestuous childhood, however, intense anger can arise in response to minor frustrations. Feeling as if people are always taking advantage of them, they may go on the attack in order to "get the other guy before he gets me." Anger thus becomes a means to intimidate others rather than to express legitimate grievances.

Stuart used his anger to bully others, and he was out of control. The proprietor of a box-paper plant formerly run by his father, he frequently exploded at his employees, who, in turn, feared him. "See the way I yell and rant? That's my father's way of handling a situation. I run the business the way he ran the place. He taught me that you've got to expect the help to take advantage of you. He believed that if you were not tough, they would walk all over you."

Stuart knew that his addiction to anger dated back to childhood. In his family, interacting always involved yelling and screaming. He and his brother used to argue constantly, as did his parents, both with each other and with the children.

Stuart opted not to change. He chose to remain angry and hostile. He never learned how to relax and stay calm. This decision did come at a price as he developed high blood pressure and often did destructive things. One day he came to therapy with his hand in a bandage as the result of his having slammed it into a wall. Furthermore, he continued to make life miserable for his employees, which negatively affected his business by reducing his employees' motivation to work hard.

In contrast to Stuart, depressed people direct their anger inward, against themselves. They may also experience somatic symptoms such as headaches, back aches, and stomachaches. They often feel excessive guilt and tend to blame themselves for their own misfortune. Sometimes their depressed moods include feelings of hopelessness and helplessness and suicidal thoughts and gestures. At times, they engage in self-destructive behaviors such as overeating, excessive drinking, or other acts of self-abuse.

As opposed to Stuart's overt anger and aggressiveness, Larry was passive and nearly always deferred to others.

Larry would deny his own needs and wishes in favor of someone else's. Whenever he went out with his friends, he would do what they wanted to do—for example, see the movie they wanted to see. He rarely expressed his feelings and kept all his anger bottled up inside. "I don't know why I can't tell people that I am angry. The other day, I waited twenty minutes for a parking space and a man drove right into it before I could react. What was I supposed to do, start a fight? I felt angry, but was too scared to say anything to him. After that, I felt really hopeless and depressed."

By not asserting himself, Larry avoids feeling fearful and anxious in the short-term. Furthermore, by rationalizing, he exacerbated his difficulties. His self-defeating behavior, however, took its toll in the form of his depressed mood, his fleeting thoughts of suicide, and his bodily aches and pains. He had not yet figured out that he had been unhappy his whole life.

As a child, Larry's mother used to talk harshly about "fresh kids" and warned him to be polite and behave properly. Still hearing his mother's injunctions that, "You can catch more flies with honey," "you should not speak unless you are spoken to," and "don't talk back—it's rude," he has been conditioned to always be cooperative. Unfortunately, his attempt to "be a good kid" is ruining his life as an adult.

Self-Reflection Questions

What can make you feel angry? How often do you experience anger? In what ways does it interfere with your daily functioning? Do you ever become violent? Or do you hold your anger inside? Do you ever experience physical symptoms, such as stomachaches or headaches, when angry?

What can make you feel depressed? How often do you experience a depressed mood? In what ways does it interfere with your daily functioning? Do you ever feel physical symptoms such as fatigue or body pains, when depressed?

Chapter Three

UNCOVERING THE SOURCE

As the examples in the previous chapter demonstrate, very often, the problems that plague us in adulthood had their beginnings many years earlier, during childhood. It is well established that parents significantly affect the development of their children. Our upbringing plays a large role in determining our self perception, confidence, and how we relate to people. Our relationships with our parents become a model for all our experiences. This early model forms the basis of our personality and dictates how we respond to a variety of situations. In other words, as adults, on some level, we still assume that everyone, and everything, will react to us just as our parents did. Although we may have forgotten about our early years, our model still affects our thoughts and behaviors as adults.

Individuals are usually unaware that their models from childhood are not perfect guides to the real world, and are therefore led astray by false preconceptions that can cause considerable anxiety. Because of these early models fostered by parental relationships, people confuse what *has* happened to them with what *will* happen to them. Rather than realizing that they were dealt some "bad cards" in childhood, and that things could be much different as adults, they expect continued disappointment because that is what they became used to as children. They know no other way. All too often they become discouraged and fail to take advantage of opportunities. In contrast, I encourage you to make sense of your past and keep an open mind about the future. The more we understand about our childhoods and our early parental models of attachment, the more freedom we have to act in new and exciting ways.

How Were You Programmed as a Child?

In order to change and grow, you will need to understand how your relationships with your parents have affected you.

Barbara's strict father all too often directed his emotional outbursts at her when she was a child. As an adult, she had difficulty dating because, deep down, she felt that no man could be trusted. She had a pattern of jumping from one brief fling to the next. Slowly, as she realized how hurt she felt by her father's behavior, she began to let her guard down and explore more intimate relationships. Her painful history with her father had kept her stuck until she put all the pieces together.

Don't be surprised if you find that processing your childhood experiences is emotionally challenging. You need to do this work in stages. Begin by filling out the Childhood Log (Exercise 1) about your parental relationships. The survey includes listing three positive aspects about your relationship with each parent (include any stepparents, foster parents, or significant parental figures in your life). Then list three negative aspects about your relationship with each parent (include any stepparents). Would you raise your children as you were raised? Why or why not? Feel free to use additional paper if needed.

Exercise 1: Childhood Log

A: List 3 positive aspects of your relationship with each parent or step parent:

(step) Mother 1. _____
                2. _____
                3. _____
(step) Father 1. _____
                2. _____
                3. _____

B: List 3 negative aspects of your relationship with each parent or step parent:

(step) Mother 1. _____
                2. _____
                3. _____
(step) Father 1. _____
                2. _____
                3. _____

C: Would you raise your children as you were raised?

Why?   _____

            _____

Why Not?   _____

            _____

Now think about your answers to the questionnaire. Did you learn anything new? Did any feelings surface as a result of recording your responses? It is important to stay aware of your thoughts and feelings as you move through this process. They will be your guide. This awareness will make it possible for you to change your life in a variety of positive ways.

As you respond to the questionnaires in this book, you will identify areas in your life that are unsatisfying. You may be having difficulty with passivity, aggression, jealousy, or procrastination. Whatever you find is the problem, it is important to realize that you are likely not at fault for its original development, but are the one who has the capacity and the responsibility to change it. You will need to learn why you have fallen into such traps. In most cases, childhood misfortunes beyond your control lead to an unhealthy pattern of behavior. Self-defeating behaviors are "false friends." They enable you to avoid unpleasant memories, thoughts, and feelings, but do not lead to understanding or resolving the problem.

> Laura, the mother of three, lived a very passive life when it came to asserting herself in relationships. As long as she remained passive with her husband, Arthur, she did not have to face the depth of her childhood frustrations, both with her parents and early childhood experiences. Standing up for herself would have activated thoughts about the frightening times of her early life. Her parents would yell and scream at each other, often throwing things in violent tirades. As a young child, she was terrified by these experiences. Her parents were so involved in their relationship and its problems that they ignored the needs of their child.

Laura was truly helpless to act. She always believed that her needs were not as important as those of the others around her because that is what her parents' actions taught her. As an adult, however, she does have considerably more strength and ability to act upon her environment than she realizes.

By being passive, she normalizes her unhappiness. She sends herself the message that just as it was once okay for her parents to ignore her needs, it is okay for Arthur to ignore them now. She is telling herself that this is just life. She doesn't see that a set of early misfortunes has forced her to feel powerless and ineffectual. She is accepting what she thinks she deserves. While Laura's passivity helps her to avoid feelings of anxiety, sadness, and loss dating back to childhood, her adult life is severely compromised. She boxes herself into a prison of her own making, thinking that things can be no other way. She doesn't see that she has options.

I hope you have a greater insight into why it is so important to trace your problems back through your history. Without the awareness of why certain patterns of behavior developed, it can be harder to change them. If Laura could clearly see the origin of her passivity, she may well be on her way to changing her behavior patterns. She must realize that her parents were unable to take care of her needs and tend to her appropriately due to their own conflictual relationship and not because she did anything wrong. She'll be well on her way to a happier and more fulfilling future when she is able to make this insight. Once Laura can understand that her needs are very important, just as important as anyone else's, she will be able to assert herself and feel greater confidence.

Can you see how things might be very different for Laura if she could understand where her passivity stemmed from?

Passive Is Not the Way to Go

Self-defeating behaviors typically have their roots in childhood misfortunes that have not been worked through. For example, Laura confuses her fears about the past with those about the present. Because she has not processed her feelings from childhood, she carries them around in her current life as a wife and mother. Rather than asserting herself in these adult roles, she remains stuck in a behavior dating back to childhood. While her passivity may have been necessary for her survival in her family, it is an obstacle in her adult life.

Self-defeating roles may be tempting because they help control unpleasant emotions associated with both the past and the future. Being passive also protects Laura from the unknown. She mistakenly equates behaving differently with disaster. She fears that if she expressed her desire for more intimacy to Arthur, he would explode in anger. That is what her parents did when (as a child) she made requests of them. In actuality, Arthur may or may not be responsive to her request, but change requires taking some risks. What Laura needs to do is take some action in order to improve the situation. Perhaps Arthur can come around to some degree. She will never know if she remains passive. If Arthur proves particularly rejecting, at least she knows where she stands. In that case, she might need to consider what life might be like without him. She may not want to end the marriage, but she needs to explore all her options. Unfortunately, Laura is not assessing the situation accurately. She associates the status quo with her own survival. In fact, taking action is not as dangerous as she thinks. The one thing that is guaranteed is that change will never occur if she remains passive.

While a combination of heredity and environment influence the persons we become, we need to pay particular attention to our childhood experiences. In contrast to adults who grow up in supportive families, adults traumatized or trained to look at themselves negatively as children report much higher levels of emotional distress. Early negative experiences have the power to impair our growth and function as adults.

Whatever particular misfortunes you experienced in your formative years made an imprint on you. Just as more overt kinds of parental misbehavior harm children, so do more subtle ones. In my clinical experience, nearly all adults who take on self-defeating patterns struggle with unhappy childhood memories. Many of my patients typically had parents who meant well, but who were unable to provide sufficient emotional support. They grew up in families where their parents fought a lot with each other, or where they were subjected to excessive criticism and name-calling. Likewise, their parents may not have been completely trustworthy or may have overprotected them. Unfortunately, these patterns of parental behavior, which have not been as widely researched as outright abuse, are all too common. Parents are usually unaware of the enormous impact of all their words and actions. To a dependent, sensitive, vulnerable child, parents are godlike figures who constitute the center of his/her universe. Children believe what they are told by these trusted adults. If their parents tell them they are dumb and worthless, children feel that they *are* dumb and worthless. After all, their parents wouldn't say it unless it were true. As adults, still feeling the strong effects of negative words, they may engage in self-defeating and self-destructive behavior patterns.

Children have no choice but to internalize what their parents tell them.

> Alan, for example, began to feel he was stupid after his mother kept putting him down. He also felt rejected and alone. "I figured that I shouldn't try to go to college if I was so stupid. In the final analysis, I was stupid to believe the name my mother was calling me."

Sorting through your childhood does not entail uncovering unpleasant experiences for their own sake. As a matter of fact, you are going back to the past in order to clear out all those negative messages from your head. Ultimately, if you make a commitment to change, you can free yourself from your childhood wounds. As an adult, you cannot change what happened many years ago, but you can reduce the hold that painful experiences have on you today.

Now that you have a deeper understanding of how negative experiences in childhood can have lasting effects in adulthood, it is your turn to try to uncover the source of your problems. Once you trace your behavior patterns to their origins, you will have a much easier time combating the negative thoughts and behaviors that you are trying to rid yourself of. Additionally, you will find it much easier to change and move toward the life that you've always wanted. On the next page you'll find the childhood misfortune checklist (Exercise 2). Fill out this questionnaire as completely and thoroughly as possible. Check all the items that apply to you, describing the specific circumstances where appropriate. For example, if you were verbally abused, note at what age it started, what form the abuse took, and how you processed it at the time. Use extra sheets of paper if necessary.

Exercise 2: Childhood Misfortune Checklist

Misfortune   Specific Circumstances/Comments

☐ 1.   Neglect_____

☐ 2.   Verbal abuse_____

☐ 3.   Physical abuse _____

☐ 4.   Sexual Abuse_____

☐ 5.   Abandonment (including premature death of a parent)
_____

☐ 6.   Parental drug or alcohol abuse_____

☐ 7.   Parental divorce _____

☐ 8.   Overprotection by one or both parents
_____

☐ 9.   Parental criticism _____

☐ 10. Excessive parental expectations _____

☐ 11. Favoritism expressed for a sibling _____

☐ 12. Traumatic experience outside the home
_____

☐ 13. Extended illness _____

☐ 14. Other _____

Identifying the misfortunes that you endured in childhood may bring up some painful and uncomfortable feelings. At times people seeking change will protect themselves from facing these wounds by denying that there was a problem.

For example, Laura minimizes the effects of her parents' mistreatment by saying: "I never felt safe with them, but it wasn't so bad because they were usually yelling at each other, not me. Well, I guess my dad did yell at me a lot, but that's all in the past now; it doesn't matter. Arthur's the problem now, not my father. At least my father always worked hard to provide for us."

Change often requires peeling away this emotional defense and developing a more realistic view of your parents' behaviors. I am urging you not to criticize your parents for the sake of finding fault or a place to lay blame. Your intention should be to improve your store of self-knowledge about the relationship of your past to your present. The goal of exploring your childhood is to trace the history of problems. You may not be able to make any connections right away. As mentioned earlier, people often resist identifying deeply rooted patterns because of the potential pain involved. This process takes time and patience.

Survival Strategy

Whatever childhood misfortunes you experienced, they backed you into a corner. As a child, you may not have been able to function with the knowledge that some important needs were not being met by the adults whose love and support you depended on. Most children develop a survival strategy that enables them to attend to activities at school and home, while putting aside the emotions associated with stress in the family.

Self-defeating behaviors emerge as part of this survival strategy. They provide an environment where you run risks if you express yourself directly. However, though they may have been adaptive to the world of your childhood, they are ill-suited to your needs as an adult.

Patients frequently ask if it is necessary to "drag up all that junk" from childhood. They may know full well exactly what misfortunes they had to endure as children, but prefer not to think about them. Sometimes, people even assume that processing these experiences will make them feel more depressed and inadequate.

Coming to terms with any of the items on the childhood misfortune checklist happens in stages. It is rare that people have a great revelation in which they are cured after uncovering a traumatic experience. In reality, recovery involves

(1) identifying exactly what has happened, (2) noting how it has affected you, (3) working through your anger, sadness and grief, and (4) engaging in healthier modes of behavior. This sorting out requires time and energy, but you will be well rewarded for your efforts. As you begin to connect your fears and anxieties to past situations, you will free yourself from the need to act according to old scripts and tapes. Gradually, you will find the courage to act in ways that promote your long-term health and well-being.

We all like to feel that we are in control, and getting rid of self-defeating roles means facing some scary truths. Children have little control over their lives. Although they can be made to feel they deserve any mistreatment that they receive from the adults in their environments, in reality, all children deserve love and support. As adults, we need to empathize with ourselves and realize that we did what we had to do as children, even if that meant adopting self-defeating roles. As adults, we do, in fact, have much greater control, but we often fail to avail ourselves of it. By clarifying the difference between how we _had_ to behave then and how we _can_ behave now, we can define new roles for ourselves that enhance the quality of our lives.

Gary grew up with an unpredictable mother. Most of the time, she was easygoing, but every once in a while, her anger got out of control. She would yell and call him "a rotten kid." When he was a child, Gary had no choice but to listen to his mother's explosions without responding. Sadly, when he tried to approach his father for support, his father snapped at him for his tendency to "upset his mother."

As an adult, Gary was meek and felt uncomfortable around people. In his forties, he had never married and earned his living as a watch repairman. He would daydream about being more connected to others as he worked in isolation in a jewelry store. One day, the building that housed the store burned down. Gary was out of a job. Due to changes in the watch industry, he couldn't find another one. He started therapy in the hope of developing some vocational plans. Once in treatment, Gary realized that his problems extended beyond the workplace. Because of his mother's verbal abuse, he felt enormous anxiety whenever he would try to assert himself. His mother had labeled him "selfish" and "argumentative" simply for expressing his own needs and concerns.

Isolating himself and avoiding social relationships, Gary kept himself from re-experiencing memories of his mother's tirades, but it also left him unable to take control of his life. Gradually, he learned that he was more afraid of what had already happened to him than what might happen now. By sorting out his thinking, he developed more confidence in social settings. Gary ended up taking a position as a salesperson, a job he used to fear. He began to feel sad about how his mother had treated him and about the fifteen years that he had spent repairing watches: "I'm so relieved that I got out of that prison. It took a fire to get me going, but at least I am living again. I like the new 'me,' and I am never going back. Now I am constantly sizing up situations, looking for new ways to be assertive."

The ultimate purpose of uncovering the source of the undesirable patterns in your life is to give yourself the opportunity to learn new ways of relating to others. Once Gary understood his behavior and the experiences that led to them, he could create a positive identity for himself. A natural disaster, such as a fire, should not be necessary for you to step out of your self-defeating patterns.

While completing the checklist concerning your childhood misfortunes may have made you uncomfortable, you now understand why it is important to work through experiences you endured in childhood. You may have explored your early relationships and experiences and have been unable to relate them to your unresolved problems. That is okay. Maybe a connection will come to you at a different time. If you do not remember, are blocking out unpleasant memories, or just can't seem to trace them back to childhood, you can still change your life and be the person you want to be. It is not necessary to find the origins of the problem, but it does help the process of change if you can.

We can *never* change what happened to us in the past. However, we can change how our past affects us today. By courageously facing some painful events in your past, you are giving yourself the opportunity to create a brighter future for yourself.

These first three chapters were intended to give a broader understanding of what may hold you back from being emotionally stronger and capable of facing problems directly. The powerful influence of parents on the growth and development of a child was discussed so that you will be encouraged to note what your parental tapes are. The common core effects of guilt, negative thinking, poor self-concept, lack of initiative, and anger/depression were presented as what effects may prevail when an individual's emotional needs are not met. You were asked to reflect on your particular background experiences. I hope insights emerged that elicited a deeper understanding of why you may be unhappy, unhealthy, or unfulfilled. Having these insights will be instrumental in guiding you as you move along your personal peace process.

PART TWO

GEARING UP

Chapter Four

IDENTIFYING RESISTANCE

Well-adjusted people are not people who never have any problems; contrarily, they are people who have just as many problems as you or I. The difference is that they deal with their problems before the problems become bigger and debilitating, rather than avoiding them, hoping they'll go away by themselves. Chances are, if you are dealing with big or nagging problems, you have been using specific styles of coping without being aware of them. In this chapter, I will discuss resistance in terms of *coping styles*, or particular thought patterns and behaviors that people typically engage in to avoid change. Many of these represent *defense mechanisms*, which we rely on to guard against anxious feelings. Defense mechanisms are common behaviors that deny or distort reality, thus keeping us "safe."

Most people, when faced with the opportunity to follow new paths of behavior, experience at least some amount of resistance. Resistance has to do with all that is in opposition to emotional growth. Specifically, it refers to attitudes, ideas, feelings, and actions that distract a person from pursuing change. It is natural that individuals want to stick with what is known, safe, and comfortable because these familiar patterns seem to make them feel secure. Any kind of path into the unfamiliar is often anxiety provoking. In my practice of psychotherapy, I strive to help patients overcome the anxiety associated with change, to open new paths of thought and behavior. When this occurs, patients can experience healthier, more satisfying emotions. To do this, the therapist points out to the patient ways in which he or she is demonstrating resistance, and attempts to interpret the reasons behind them. Only then can individuals begin to deal with their resistance.

It may seem strange that patients who have committed themselves to the process of self-understanding would impede their own progress with resistance. However, it is not surprising when you realize that humans do not want to experience painful feelings, and often are not optimistic regarding their ability to change. Perhaps the most important point to keep in mind when embarking on a new road to change is that resistances do not simply represent obstacles to be overcome. They should be recognized as defenses against anxiety that interfere with the ability to

31

experience a more gratifying life. In this way, they may be viewed as signals, alerting you to the fact that you are trying to avoid something, which allows you to consider the reason and permits the opportunity to explore other ways of dealing with your anxiety. In the traditional therapy setting, resistance may be expressed in a variety of ways. For example, a patient who is confronted with painful feelings following a particularly emotional session may resist exploring those issues further by canceling the next appointment or not showing up at all. Resistance may also be manifest as tardiness with appointments or talking about trivial day-to-day events, thus avoiding any deeper discussion. Another example would be the patient's attempt to redirect the communication with the therapist so as to avoid discussing something that is upsetting.

John had been seeing me regularly for two months when we began discussing his relationship with his mother, who was killed in a car accident when he was eleven. He had avoided this topic in previous sessions and it eventually became clear to me that it brought up difficult feelings for him. Usually staid in our sessions, John became tearful and agitated when we first processed these upsetting feelings. At the end of our session, I told him that I thought we should continue talking about this topic the following week and he agreed. The next week came and went, however, with no sign of John. It took him two weeks to finally call and explain that he had been too busy to meet with me. Fortunately, when he did return, he was able to discuss how upset he had been the previous therapy session. He said he finally realized the importance of dealing with the sadness of his mother's death, no matter how painful.

IDENTIFY YOUR PRESENT COPING STYLES

Throughout my career, I have observed numerous maladaptive *styles of being*, or coping styles (see Exercise 3 at the end of this chapter). As you read through the following examples, try to identify those that might match your own behavior patterns. Most are the results of misperceptions due to poor self-esteem. As you progress along your personal peace process, I will help you to recognize and eliminate those that are causing you to live beneath your potential.

COPING STYLE #1: FAILURE TO GIVE ONESELF CREDIT WHEN CREDIT IS DUE

A number of patients habitually think they are inadequate, or failures. I often tell them that they are, in fact, failures, but not in the way they describe. Instead, they consistently fail by not internalizing their strengths. Everyone has admirable characteristics, but, unfortunately, many are blind to their own. If you seldom give yourself credit, it is like being in a business and throwing away the profit. At the end of the day you are left with nothing, and that's exactly how you feel. The only way to counter this tendency is to acknowledge your strengths and accomplishments. We will review ways of doing this in chapter five, "Finding the Courage to Change."

COPING STYLE #2: ATTACHING INCORRECT MEANING TO SITUATIONS

Jeanne was upset because her husband did not give her a card for her birthday, although he had already taken her out for dinner. She felt hurt and unappreciated. I asked her if he was a good husband, and whether she felt the absence of a card meant that he loved her any less. She smiled in recognition that her perception of the situation had been faulty, and was then able to put her reaction into perspective. Once she was able to re-evaluate the situation, Jeanne no longer felt hurt.

Only accurate perceptions can bring about accurate feelings—distortions cannot produce positive feelings. It is wise to be flexible in your thinking, since matters are not always simply right or wrong. One person's thoughts are not always better than another's; sometimes they are just different.

COPING STYLE #3: SEEKING EVIDENCES OF ONE'S OWN INFERIORITY

This example is similar to failing to give yourself credit. Before an individual can accept anything positive about life, there has to be an acknowledgment of self-worth. Too often, patients think, "That's too good for me. I don't deserve it."

Insecure people have a tendency to look for evidence of negative characteristics. They can recite a long list of shortcomings. They can tell you about a nose that's too long or a waistline that's too large, but they have difficulty finding anything good to say about themselves.

When I talk to patients who are very negative, I often utilize the mirror technique. I ask them to say whatever comes to mind, while looking in the mirror. Often times, the responses I get are the same as a patient's of mine named Maureen:

> "She is ugly ... she appears nice to people, but I wonder how sincere she is ... she's wasting her life ... her hair is a mess ... her nose is too big ... how could anyone like her?"
>
> "Indeed," I repeated to Maureen, "how could anyone like her when she doesn't like herself?" I asked Maureen to imagine that the woman she was talking to in the mirror was someone else. How did she think that other person would feel after hearing what she had said? "Pretty lousy," Maureen admitted. I pointed out to her the necessity for paying attention to the messages she sent herself. If they reinforced her perception of a poor self-image, she obviously would not view herself positively.

We will cover this concept again in chapter five, and if this is an issue for you, you will be given methods to help change your self-image from a negative one to a more realistic and positive one.

COPING STYLE #4: ANTICIPATING THE WORST POSSIBLE SCENARIO

It is difficult to help people change when they are so anxious about life that they habitually anticipate the worst or always fear losing control. One man would not come into my office unless he could bring several members of his family with him. "After all," he explained, "I feel helpless when I get nervous. If something happens to me, I'm going to need help." Nothing serious has happened to him yet, but he insists on focusing on the worst possible scenario and keeping that negative image in sharp focus. While it is important to understand that there are indeed many aspects of life that are beyond our control, it is unhealthy to anticipate doom and gloom. Doing so will only limit the movement you can make toward change and leave you in a constant state of worry.

COPING STYLE #5: ALLOWING ONE'S SYMPTOMS TO AFFECT REASON

Often times, people confuse feelings with thoughts, so that eventually they are unable to differentiate between the two.

Pamela was a successful attorney who complained constantly about her depression. "This isn't living," she would tell me. "I'd be better off dead. I'm wasting my life. I can't cope." She was so caught up in her depression that she couldn't remember why she felt down in the first place. I explained to her that the reason she felt so depressed was because she was telling herself to feel that way. "You can't feel down," I remarked, "unless you've sent negative messages to your brain. It has to register there first before you can feel anything." Once, after Pam told me she would be better off dead, I commented, "You sound like a person seeking the assistance of a mortician, not a psychologist." She smiled and shot back, "Don't be a wise guy."

She was able to see the humor in allowing her negative feelings to dictate her thinking. It is important not to give into those negative feelings; instead, find out what is producing them so that you can deal directly with the problem.

COPING STYLE #6: AVOIDING ALL TROUBLESOME SITUATIONS

Some people are masters at staying away from situations in their lives where conflict is anticipated. Kim, who is thirty-seven, has had a driver's license for twenty years, but seldom drives for fear of getting lost or having an accident. As a result, she has remained at an unfulfilling job for nine years simply because it is within walking distance of her home. Bruce, a fifty-one-year-old husband and father, is fearful of speaking before large groups. Because he is a vice president of the company, it's easy for him to delegate this task. But that solution is hardly rewarding in terms of his professional growth and development as a person. He is always fearful of being asked to speak in the future. What are you avoiding as a means of escape from anticipated problems? Strength and confidence come from facing obstacles directly and managing situations that hold you back.

COPING STYLE #7: REMAINING SILENT WHEN ONE SHOULD SPEAK

When people tell me about some conflict they are experiencing in their relationships, I often ask them, "What did you do or say?" Often they will answer, "I felt it best to say nothing," or, "I didn't want to start an argument." And when I ask, "What do you *wish* you had said?" they usually respond with something like: "I would like to tell them to go to hell!" Sometimes they tell me things that would have been most effective and appropriate had they said them to the person with whom they were interacting. There are times when people are reluctant to say what is on their minds because they think they will say something foolish or start an argument they can't handle. Well, we don't always make the wisest comments or feel we can handle an argument. Keeping quiet because you fear the consequences of speaking out is not in your best interest. It is not an effective way of dealing with a problem. It is an ineffective way to deal with a situation because no growth or lasting solution can take place. In fact, it can cause you to go backwards. You keep running over in your mind what you would like to say to the other person if only you weren't afraid. All that you accomplish by doing that is to raise the level of your fear and get angry with yourself. Even if it does cause some anxiety, it's always better to think about how or what you feel and then say what is on your mind.

DEFENSE MECHANISMS AS RESISTANCE TOOLS

Resistance does not only refer to coping styles. The various coping styles were mentioned to give you an idea of how prevalent these habits are, which makes it difficult to change. Most of these coping styles rely on defense mechanisms. Listed below are the main defense mechanisms that form the basis of our coping styles. As you read them, try to identify those that match your own behavior patterns and think about how often (or under what circumstances) you rely on each one (see Exercise 4). People needing change typically use more than one. Such maladaptive behavior provides false comfort by allowing you to stay in seemingly safe territory. In the long-term, however, these unhealthy styles can restrain you from reaching your true potential and even make your problems worse.

DEFENSE MECHANISM #1: DENIAL

Denial involves not acknowledging reality. Denial of what is obvious to others is often considered the simplest of all defense mechanisms—it is a way of distorting what an individual thinks or feels. Many people deny the existence of a problem by "closing their eyes" and letting it progress until it affects their ability to function effectively. I often hear patients state, "I'm not sure there's a reason for my being here," or "I really don't believe my problems are serious enough to bother you with."

In times of crisis, denial serves a useful purpose. When faced with a traumatic event, such as the death of a loved one, we may need to disbelieve what has happened for a while in order to process our overwhelming grief. Denial emerges as a problem only when we use it over the long haul to look past unpleasant realities in our lives, such as our own self-destructive behaviors.

> Amelia was referred to me by an officer of the court because she had been repeatedly beaten by her husband. She was still black and blue from the bruises she had received in the latest incident when I first met her. Yet her only comment was, "Yes, he hits me, but he's a steady worker and I never have to go without anything."

Here was a human punching bag who was unwilling to acknowledge the extent of her situation. Instead, she minimized the problem, in essence, remaining in denial, so as to avoid the pain involved in admitting that her life was so dissatisfactory. Additionally, she lacked the self-confidence to try to get away from her husband.

> Susan denies her gambling problem, although she makes the two-hour drive to the casino as often as she can. Furthermore, despite mounting debt, she gambles with money reserved for household expenses. Although the situation is spiraling out of control, she does not acknowledge that anything is wrong: "I can stop anytime I want," she says. And she rationalizes by adding, "I know people who spend a lot more money than I do." By denying that she has a problem, she is letting it escalate because it is easier than facing the potentially painful feelings involved with admitting that she has lost control over her gambling.

DEFENSE MECHANISM #2: AVOIDANCE

This style is the most simple and straightforward. Avoiders do everything possible not to address problems. Unlike people who are in denial about a problem, someone who avoids a situation is consciously aware of what he or she is doing. While they realize that a problem exists, they make every attempt to keep from dealing with it. Usually, avoidance occurs because of irrational fears of what might happen if a conflict is approached directly.

Richard's relationship with his wife has been deteriorating for years. "When she yells at me, I get out of the house," he says.

Unfortunately, he lacks the courage to confront his wife about their conflict. In order to grow, he needs to work on his relationship with his wife. Running away during moments of tension does not improve communication, but instead increases the mutual resentment.

DEFENSE MECHANISM #3: RATIONALIZATION

Rationalization allows the individual to explain away painful feelings related to failure or loss. In this way, it "softens the blow" that occurs in disappointments. Rationalizers are adept at explaining away their problems and convincing themselves of things with statements such as:

"Well, the situation is not so bad."
"Things could be worse."
"At least I don't have it as bad as Pablo."
"If it is meant to be, it will be"
"Change would make things worse."
"Things will get better by themselves."

Do not make excuses for acts that do not enhance the quality of your life. In the following case, Tom's rationalization was self-destructive.

Tom rationalized about his smoking habit, which was exacerbating his asthma. Despite his doctor's warning that he was endangering his life, he refused to change. He preferred to delude himself:

"I don't have trouble breathing all the time! Furthermore, my father smoked and he lived to eighty-four!"

At times, rationalization can make it easier for a person to accept the reality of a situation.

Karen had worked for her company for thirteen years. The opportunity arose to apply for a different position that represented a promotion, and although she became extremely excited by the possibility of gaining more prestige, she had reservations about being able to handle the position. While her boss and co-workers encouraged her to apply for the job, she hesitated. When she was passed over in favor of another applicant, she rationalized away her disappointment and anger by convincing herself that she didn't want the new position anyway. She stated, "I really don't want that much responsibility, plus I would have to leave all of the good friends I have where I am now."

Rationalization served to save her from painful feelings. In therapy, Karen acknowledged she had held herself back because of her lack of confidence, rather than taking the risk to grow personally and professionally.

DEFENSE MECHANISM #4: PROJECTION/ BLAME

This style can be hard to identify because people who use it often are successful in disguising their problems—sometimes even from themselves! Projection involves blaming others by attributing one's own desires to other people. Thus, upsetting feelings are viewed as belonging to someone else other than the person experiencing them.

Mickey was a high school teacher who enjoyed a good relationship with his wife. His problem was that he was sexually attracted to one of his students. When I asked him about this, he maintained that it was the student who was behaving in a seductive manner with him. By projecting his own sexual impulses onto his student, he avoided acknowledging or dealing with his own desires.

DEFENSE MECHANISM #5: DISPLACEMENT

This type of defense mechanism offers a means of coping with anxiety by shifting one's feelings. Instead of directing an emotion, such as anger, toward the person who caused it, it is often safer to displace those feelings to another individual, or a "safer target."

> Joe constantly felt intimidated by his boss, who was very condescending. However, Joe felt unable to discuss his feelings with his boss or take action to find a better, less stressful work environment. Instead, he typically returned home after work and unloaded his hostility on his children, causing them to be fearful of him.

As you read through the specific coping styles and reviewed the ways in which we use defense mechanisms, what sounded familiar? Did you discover the ways you may be perpetuating self-harming habits? It is only by challenging these habits that you will be able to change and grow.

The fact is, it is unhealthy to make excuses and to always avoid areas where risk is involved. Evaluate the risk involved to determine the benefit of trying what you have been avoiding. You should be willing to face those challenges now, because even though you may not succeed exactly how you planned, you will be stronger for having made the attempt. Somewhere inside of you, you also know that it is healthy to face your problems directly. No more denying the existence of problems. No more blaming the downfalls of your life on others or making other people's problems yours as well.

I know that the idea of confronting such habits may be scary. As mentioned before, any type of change is usually anxiety-provoking. Try to identify the various ways in which you maintain the status quo so that you can begin to explore other pathways. I am confident you will be able to pinpoint and deal with the roadblocks and realize the benefits of facing issues directly.

Exercise 3: Coping Styles

Check off any coping styles that apply to you and list examples of where you have used them. Also, try to think of any other coping styles you may rely on and describe when you have used them.

☐ 1. Failure to give oneself credit when credit is due

☐ 2. Attaching incorrect meaning to situations

☐ 3. Seeking evidences of one's own inferiority

☐ 4. Anticipating the worst possible scenario

☐ 5. Allowing one's symptoms to affect reason

☐ 6. Avoiding all troublesome situations

☐ 7. Remaining silent when one should speak

☐ 8. Other coping styles:

Exercise 4: Defense Mechanisms

Check off the defense mechanisms that apply to you and list examples of where you have used them. This may be difficult at first since defense mechanisms are often by nature subconscious or subliminal. Think back to the chapter you just read and the case studies presented to see if any similar thought or behavior patterns apply to your own situations.

☐ **1. Denial**   _____
                                     _____
                                     _____

☐ **2. Avoidance**   _____
                                     _____
                                     _____

☐ **3. Rationalization**   _____
                                     _____
                                     _____

☐ **4. Projection/Blame** _____
                                     _____
                                     _____

☐ **5. Displacement**   _____
                                     _____
                                     _____

Chapter Five

FINDING THE COURAGE
TO CHANGE

ASSESS YOUR HOPEFULNESS FOR CHANGE

In his book, *The Meaning of Life*, Dr. Victor Frankel tells about his experiences as a psychiatrist in a Nazi concentration camp during World War II. He marveled at the low suicide rate among the people in the camps, despite the life-threatening conditions under which they lived. These included the ultimate in human degradation, brutality, and sickness. Frankel attributed this phenomenon to the fact that his fellow inmates had something to look forward to—reuniting with a loved one, resuming a career, or finding freedom once again.

When it appears there is nothing to look forward to, it is not uncommon for people to feel hopeless about their prospects for change. This is especially true if they have already failed in several attempts to resolve difficult problems that have been plaguing them for years.

How hopeful are you? I encourage you to rate your hopefulness (Exercise 5) on a scale of one to ten (with one meaning "extremely hopeful," ten, "extremely hopeless," and five, "neither hopeless nor hopeful").

It is important to be as honest with yourself as possible. Feeling somewhat hopeless (or even extremely hopeless) is understandable, especially if your unhappiness has lasted for years. If your score falls anywhere in the hopeless category, do not fight your feelings, but try to persist despite them. It often helps to list all the reasons why you feel this way. In many cases, previous experiences—either in childhood or in the recent past—account for these troubling emotions. In this chapter, we will discuss how, even when things may feel hopeless at first, you can overcome your situation. Often, the first step is finding the courage to begin.

Exercise 5: Hopefulness Gauge

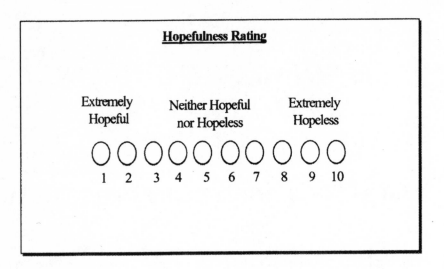

If you score 6 or above, why do you think you feel this way?

_____

_____

_____

_____

How many times have you fantasized about changing something in your life—your job, your appearance, or a relationship—but found some reason to avoid the change and instead maintain the status quo? You may have said to yourself, "I don't think change is possible" or, "It's not really a big deal, I can live with it the way it is." The fact of the matter is that all of this negative self-talk represents one basic thing: fear of change. Fortunately, we have an antidote to the fear of change, and that is courage. By developing courage, you can face your fears and move forward on your personal peace process.

Have you ever thought that changing your life would take courage? Yes, fear often accompanies major change, and overcoming fear indeed requires courage. Change need not be a terrifying experience, but it is something that will cause you to stop, assess your situation, decide what changes need to be made, and have the confidence, self-assurance, and, yes, courage to proceed with your desired goals.

We tend to be comfortable with what is familiar to us, even though it may cause great emotional pain and unhappiness. Therefore, we resist change because it represents the unfamiliar. There are some people who embrace the unfamiliar and thrive on change, never satisfied to remain a certain way for too long. For the majority of people, however, this way of life is utterly foreign. Most people attempt to avoid change until they are forced to change. They fool themselves into thinking that something negative in their lives is beyond their control or is a situation they are just stuck with. They learn to live with things the way they are, thus existing below their true potential.

Your own self-concept has a great deal to do with your ability to face your fears. If you feel a strong sense of self-worth and believe in yourself, you are able to stand firm and proceed toward the desired changes with confidence. There will be less fear because you will believe that what you are doing is in your own best interests, and that *you* are important. Believing in yourself and seeking the best possible life should be your goal. Seek the challenges and rewards that result from change.

Chris worked as a mechanic for a small auto shop. He was skilled at his trade and produced fine work for his boss. He stayed on the job despite long hours, poor fringe benefits, and less than adequate pay because he was afraid to explore other jobs. The boss was overly critical and constantly badgered Chris without cause. As a result, Chris had come to believe that he would not be capable of working at another job, and, instead, convinced himself he was fortunate to have the job he had!

TAKE SMALL STEPS

Because Chris lacked the self-confidence needed to obtain a new position, he was encouraged to take small steps toward making a change. For example, he agreed to ask around to friends in the same profession so as to find out how marketable he was. In this way, Chris took the first step—he surveyed other positions he might qualify for. He found that there were indeed a number of available positions, and with additional encouragement he submitted his application to various companies. As it turned out, Chris was hired by a large car dealer at twice the salary he'd been making.

It took Chris courage to change jobs. For years, he had rationalized that he had no control over his job situation, so he had stayed on despite being unhappy. He did this because it was easier than facing the unfamiliar. Uncovering the unfamiliar, however, by exploring other job options, gave him the courage to move on. When we can explore the unfamiliar terrain without risking our own emotional safety, often times change comes about naturally as the next step. This occurs because the unfamiliar is no longer mysterious or foreboding. Instead, it is usually seen as an exciting new frontier to be discovered!

Iris was an independent, successful executive secretary. Although she was happy with her work and her social relationships, she complained that she felt guilty whenever she was with her mother. "My mother is very hard to please," she explained. "Her usual comments whenever I see her are, 'To what do we owe the honor of this visit?' or, 'You could call me once in a while to see if I'm alive.'" Her mother's comments resulted in Iris feeling like a bad child and reminded her of all the hurt feelings she had suffered growing up.

I encouraged Iris to imagine what would happen if she cut back on her visits altogether. She realized that many of her visits were the result of her feeling guilty. Finally, when she came to the conclusion that her mother could never be a supportive, encouraging, understanding person in her life, Iris stopped trying to please her. She had realized that she too was an adult and did not need to depend on her mother for love the way she did as a child. It took courage for Iris to stand on her own feet and take control of the matter. She developed this courage only after viewing her relationship with her mother from a different perspective. She mentally "tested the waters" by imagining how her relationship with her mother would be if she took action rather than maintaining a passive role. Once she saw that those "waters" were relatively safe, she was able to jump in. She now visits her mother when she feels like it, and she only stays as long as she wishes. Iris is no longer influenced by her mother's need to produce guilt. Instead, she now has the courage to face the relationship on her terms.

I asked Iris what gave her the strength to grow emotionally apart from her mother.

She said, "You made me aware of the fact that my mother was never going to be accepting and supporting. You said I was waiting for a bus that would never come. I guess I finally realized you were right."

No matter where you see yourself on the self-esteem continuum, changing your life does require some amount of genuine courage, sometimes more and sometimes less, depending on how vast the goal. If you normally drink eight cups of caffeinated coffee a day and want to quit, tapering down from eight cups to six cups at first will not seem as frightening as quitting cold turkey. Breaking up with a girlfriend or boyfriend after one month may not feel as life changing as divorcing after a fifteen-year marriage. Varying amounts of courage may be called for depending on the goal. It is often easier to summon up the courage to take a small step than to take a deep plunge.

ACKNOWLEDGE YOUR STRENGTHS

Generally, people find it easier to talk about their inadequacies rather than their strengths. Don't be afraid to think about what is strong and good about yourself. If you see yourself as helpless, it will be extremely difficult to ever believe that you are a person of great worth. But it is possible! Do not give up. Do not give into your self-defeating negative thoughts and fears.

Lila, a sixty-year-old mother of three was referred to me because of severe depression. I found her to be a highly dependent woman who, in her later years, had become increasingly frightened. She worried that her children didn't like her, she worried about illness, she worried that her husband would leave her, and she worried about people not wanting to share her company. What Lila did not acknowledge was that she was an educated woman who'd successfully raised three contributing children and maintained positions of importance in her church and other local community groups.

When you adopt a host of negative labels, it is unlikely that you will ever see yourself as a person worthy of being loved or having close friendships.

People can imprison themselves with their fears by reducing the size and scope of their world through negative thoughts and behaviors. If you are afraid of failure and rejection, don't stay in solitary confinement in some prison of your imagination. The rewards of being free and experiencing peace of mind are too valuable to place in jeopardy by giving into fears. Be courageous. And don't you think you will be more courageous if you think of yourself as the strong, accomplished person that you are, instead of focusing your own self-image on your perceived short-comings?

GET RID OF NEGATIVE MESSAGES

Fear of change represents self-doubt in disguise. This leads you to hold yourself back from what you truly desire. Our fears are those negative tapes that play over and over in our heads. Those thoughts causing self-doubts did not originate with us. They are old messages that we heard from authority figures, parents, teachers, peers, coaches, and relatives. Perhaps you heard such statements as, "You're not good enough" or, "You'll never succeed." These negative messages are designed to hold you back and keep you from having the fullest life you can. Even if these exact words were never overtly expressed to you, you may have interpreted other words or actions as expressing the same idea.

The negative messages that contribute to remaining passive and maintaining the status quo can be altered. The key to doing this is to understand their source. Many of my patients had parents or significant people in their lives who meant well but were unable to provide sufficient emotional support. Either these people were not entirely trustworthy, or may have overprotected them. Too often, parents are unaware of the enormous impact of their words and actions on the developing child. Children have no choice but to internalize the messages that their parents send them. If a child receives negative parental messages, those negative tapes often carry into adulthood. These negative messages become fixed in the individual's mind causing self-doubt.

Unfortunately, even as an adult, you cannot change what happened to you many years ago. You can, however, reduce the hold that painful experiences have on you today. You can do this by understanding the ways in which negative messages serve to restrain you from making changes. They unnecessarily hold you back by making you believe that you cannot attempt change because the risk of failure is so high. Therefore, it is important that you free yourself from these negative thoughts. You must learn to see these negative statements not as your own, but as ideas that were imposed upon you when you were too young to disagree. You are now an adult, not a dependent child, and you have the ability to rid yourself of these thoughts and make change a possibility. Understanding that your negative messages did not originate from your own thoughts can help you in summoning up the courage needed to face the fears that stand in your way.

SEEK OPPORTUNITIES TO GROW

You can also overcome the hold that previous experiences have on you now by learning how to fortify yourself against life's disappointments and failures. It is important to realize that although you may have summoned up the courage to change, it is not guaranteed that you won't fail at something you've chosen to focus your energy on. We all know that nothing in life is foolproof. Therefore, if you can realize that no one can be successful at all times, it will be easier for you to overcome those times when you take a chance and it doesn't work out exactly as you planned. If you make an effort to do something for yourself and are unsuccessful, that doesn't mean you are a failure as a person. Yes, you will feel disappointed, but try to go beyond that feeling and see the situation as an opportunity to learn and grow.

LISTEN TO YOURSELF

"I have been married to my husband for seven years and it has been seven years of misery. I know I married the wrong man," said Wania, a thirty-two-year-old patient of mine. "We do not have anything to say to each other. He spends his life on the sofa watching television. We have no friends. We don't do anything interesting. He doesn't read or have any interests."

"Why did you marry him?" I asked.

"I am not sure. I thought I loved him and that he would grow up and change. Unfortunately, that never happened."

Wania went on to tell me the reason she came for help at that particular time.

> "I am in a conflict situation in more than one way. I am in love with my boss. He is everything my husband is not. He is intelligent, kind, considerate, and loving. We share a beautiful relationship together. To complicate things more, my boss wants me to divorce my husband and marry him. He has been patient, but says he can't wait forever."
>
> "What is your conflict? Why do you stay with your husband?" I asked Wania.
>
> "I am a religious person. My uncle is a priest. I could not begin to expect my mother to accept a divorce."

I realized how conflicted Wania was and understood the personal stress she was experiencing. She was torturing herself by staying in a failed marriage and denying herself a future with a man she loved because of what others would think.

Very often, people are afraid to make changes because they worry about how their friends and family will react. When obeying the wishes of society or authority figures at the expense of your own self-worth, nobody benefits. By not trusting or listening to your own inner voice of good judgment, you are setting yourself up for depression and self-blame. What's wrong with making a realistic assessment of who we are, who we want to be, and the goals we want to reach? Why can't we strive for goals that are meaningful to us rather than the people around us? Too many people go through life without ever discovering their unique qualities and gifts as human beings. They may seem to be accomplishing a lot, but in truth they are miserable doing it.

Listening to yourself is critical. However, sometimes you have to sort through which one of your voices is the appropriate one to listen to. Years ago, I saw a man whose health was in jeopardy because he smoked too much. He was having difficulty breathing and he knew he had to quit smoking. At the same time, he readily admitted his fondness for cigarettes.

My patient's feelings about his smoking habit were obviously both positive and negative. He had conflicting urges. Such dual messages can be quite confusing, for it is impossible to go in two directions at once. Whether one decides to go to a movie or play tennis may seem inconsequential, but deciding whether to apply for a new job or stay with your old job is a different issue altogether. You might ask yourself, "I would like the job, but will I be hired?" The decision to go ahead will probably be affected by your feelings of self-worth. The more confident person will at least apply; the less confident one won't.

> Although Don is not happy with his work, he stays with the job because of the inner messages he sends himself: "You are not a CPA

... be happy you are in the accounting field at all ... you are forty-nine ... not too many companies will hire you ... don't start trouble by looking for a better job ..." Simultaneously, another fainter voice is operating within Don. It should be stronger, but Don's self-concept won't let it be much of a dominant force. It says, "I know I'm not so bad ... sometimes I come up with good ideas ... I know I'm worth more money and should leave this place ..."

Because of Don's poor self-image, the first set of messages overpowers the second. As a result, Don stays with the same job and his unhappiness and frustrations continue. Listen to yourself, but listen to your *healthy self.*

THE BENEFIT OF FEAR

As with many negative emotions, fear of change can serve a purpose. The trick is to learn how to approach fear from a different perspective so that you can eventually appreciate its value. Let me explain. As with resistance, which we talked about in the previous chapter, fear can also serve as a message to ourselves. In this way, fear can actually be a friend, not an enemy. Usually, fear serves to stand in the way of progress toward our goals. Once a person feels fearful, too often, they find excuses to avoid facing the fear, so in this way fear acts like a roadblock. Instead of experiencing fear as a roadblock, the emotionally balanced person often perceives fear as a signal that makes them stop, assess the situation, evaluate the risks involved, and maintain the confidence to proceed. This may sound much easier said than done. At first it will seem very difficult. With practice, however, it will become second nature. Let's take an example.

Jim was a successful corporate lawyer who came to me because he was having difficulty getting up in the morning and functioning on the job. He was depressed and unable to feel that he was productive and successful. He admitted that he had originally chosen to practice law because he thought it would be lucrative, and because he knew it would please his family. Unfortunately, however, he disliked most aspects of his profession—he felt the hours were too long, the work was tedious, and he couldn't see how his efforts made a positive contribution to society.

When I asked him if there were any other professions he would prefer, he stated he had always loved teaching, and thought he would make a good high school teacher. Questioned as to why he didn't pursue this career, he listed a number of reasons why he couldn't, such as drastically cutting his salary and possibly disappointing his family. While these reasons were indeed valid, I pointed out to him that, in short, he was fearful of making a career change because it represented a different lifestyle. I encouraged him to keep these factors in mind, yet at the same time come up with ways in which his life would be positively changed if he were to become a teacher. He was able to acknowledge numerous positive changes that could occur if he changed his career, such as more room for creativity, contact with a younger generation, and, perhaps most appealing to him, summers off!

I encouraged him to assess the advantages and disadvantages involved with making a career change. In other words, he was pressed to consider the pros and cons of the decision and weigh them against each other: was he willing to trade a very high salary for the possibility that he could have an effect on the development of teenagers? Was the promise of summers off worth returning to school to become certified as a teacher? Did he feel confident that he could return to the law if, for some reason, he changed his mind along the way? By weighing the potential costs and benefits of making such a change, Jim was able to feel more comfortable in facing the fears involved in considering a different career. In confronting his fear of change, he was able to evaluate the situation with a clear head, which resulted in the courage to make a dramatic change in his life and pursue a new career.

Jim was able to make a major life change because he evaluated the risks involved in this type of change. Even though he acknowledged that there would be challenges along the way, he was willing to face them. This willingness did not come easily, however. Before making his decision, Jim voiced his concerns about what the consequences would be if he failed in his attempt to become a teacher. For example, although he was confident that he could manage the courses needed to become certified in teaching, he worried whether he would, in fact, be able to find a job as a teacher. This was a realistic concern, so I encouraged him to thoroughly research the employment possibilities. Jim realized that by making a career change, he might not succeed exactly as he had planned. Nevertheless, because his self-esteem was relatively intact, he understood that even if he failed in some way, he would have the courage to face the remaining challenges, such as finding a job.

Jim actually became a teacher. It took a great deal of courage for him to make such a drastic career change, especially when it meant a change in salary and lifestyle. He knew there were risks involved, but felt strongly that the rewards were worth the risk. Even though he was first fearful of making a move, his fear acted as a friend, not an enemy. With some help, he was able to take the signal from his fear, evaluate his risks, assess his options, understand the pros and cons, and develop a course of action that had contingencies for various risks. Jim has never been happier or more personally fulfilled than he is while teaching. His feelings of personal pride have never been so high.

COME TO YOUR OWN RESCUE

Treat yourself in a way that makes you feel a sense of self-respect. Don't resist positive change. If you want to resist something, resist the temptation to put yourself down and treat yourself poorly and without respect. If someone were berating your best friend, you would surely come to his or her rescue and help to stop the verbal assault. Now you have to start coming to your own rescue. Don't allow yourself to be abused by your own negative thoughts. Resist avoiding your problems. Resist bad habits that can overcome your life, ruin your health, or even kill you. Resist all of those thoughts, feelings, and behavior patterns that produce nothing but a lack of self-respect.

RAISE YOUR CONFIDENCE LEVEL

Remember, those doubts that assail you when you seek change are mostly created by your unconscious mind, which is trying to protect you from further hurt and rejection. Don't let these doubts keep you from moving ahead. For each time you make a change for the better, you become stronger and more confident. Make such changes often enough and your self-confidence will become a powerful force. But give in to your fears and you will build more fear. Fear begets fear; confidence begets confidence. Instead of immediately responding to change with fear, send yourself the positive message that you need all types of experiences to become a stronger person. Think of having an imaginary confidence meter in your brain. Every time you do something healthy, it registers positively and your self-esteem climbs. Every time you fail to treat yourself the best way possible, the meter needle falls.

I remember working in a vegetable market during my high school days, and one of my regular customers was Vince Lombardi, who later became the legendary coach of the Green Bay Packers football team. At the time, he was coaching football at nearby St. Cecilia's High School in Englewood, New Jersey. Lombardi's natural ability to reach young people quickly became apparent to me, for he invariably would stop by the market to purchase pears and apples and ask me about my plans for the future, which, I have to admit, were almost nonexistent at the time. The truth is, I was unable to think much past the immediate present. Like so many high school youngsters during World War II, I wasn't making too many plans beyond entering the army or navy.

Sensing my lack of purpose, Coach Lombardi gave me some good ideas to think about later on. "Whatever you plan to do," he told me, "do a good job. Don't settle for anything less." I've always tried to follow that philosophy, and it has served me well. Later, when it was announced that Lombardi had been named coach at Fordham University, I congratulated him. Perhaps aware that he wouldn't be stopping by so often, he said to me, "I know you haven't had much success in school, but don't give up the idea of education."

Then this great man said something I will never forget. "Kenny, you should do something for and with people." How in the world did he know I was wired for a career of working for and with people? I was a seventeen-year-old youngster who was failing four out of six subjects in high school. When, later, Lombardi had gained fame and success, I knew that one of the major reasons had to be his ability to build confidence in young men. He surely gave me confidence at a time when my educational objectives were minimal.

SOMETIMES MOUNTAINS ARE ACTUALLY JUST MOLE HILLS

Rita was a very competent nurse who enjoyed her work immensely. Unfortunately, her father was suffering from a degenerative disease and needed hospitalization full-time. She came to my office seeking advice on how to handle her conflicting desires to work and also care for her father. As we talked, the subject turned to Rita's work in the operating room. The more I listened to her, the more I felt certain that this intelligent woman was a natural candidate for medical school. When I mentioned this possibility to her, however, she became quite anxious. She explained that, while she had always wanted to attend medical school and become a surgeon, her family depended on her income, especially now that her father was unable to work. She feared giving up her senior nurse's status for the life of a lowly medical student. She was further frightened that she had no guarantee that she had the ability to get accepted to medical school and succeed as a physician.

I assured Rita that her doubts were normal and reminded her that she had already been successful in whatever she'd attempted. Then I asked her my favorite question: "What's the worst thing that could happen? And how realistic is that fear?" Those are such important questions to ask yourself when you are afraid of something. You often find that the worst thing you can think of really isn't that bad, or isn't very likely to happen.

Rita is now a surgeon. She is so proud that she had the courage to grow and change, even in the face of adversity. Of course, Rita's success didn't happen magically. It came about with a great deal of planning and effort on Rita's part. But the most important lesson is that what initially seemed to be insurmountable was actually quite achievable once she acknowledged what she wanted, set up a plan, and found the courage to begin moving.

THERE'S NO TIME LIKE THE PRESENT

I have often heard people say things like, "I'm going to start reading more when my work schedule calms down" or, "When I retire I am going to go all over the world." Excuses, excuses! It will likely never happen if you put it off. There was a time when I didn't think I could get away from my busy work schedule to travel. My family pulled me away from my office for a week and we traveled to Bethlehem and Jerusalem. The sights were fascinating and beyond description. We explored caves, climbed mountains, and swam in the Dead Sea. Some fellow vacationers were not able to participate fully because the physical activity was too strenuous, given their age. The lesson here is simple: If there is something you want to do that is really important to you, do it now while you can still make the most of the experience. Don't wait for the sunset to check out the view: it may be too dark when you get there.

LEMONADE FROM LEMONS

Sometimes you can transform the things that cause anxiety into those that make you relaxed, happy, or even excited.

Steve was referred to me because he experienced considerable anxiety waiting on the customers who visited the small gift shop he inherited. He was a very shy man who was terrified of failure. He would sit in the back room for hours and let his assistants handle the business. I decided to try to shock Steve out of this mode of behavior by announcing to him one day, "The solution to your problem is to sell the store!"

"I can't do that!" he exclaimed. "What else would I do?"

Then I told Steve that I did not really like my suggestion either, but if he insisted on the same behavior, he might as well sell the shop. The only way he could change was to recognize that he had to alter his thoughts and actions when it came to running his store. As terrifying as this seemed to him, Steve accepted the premise that, to gain confidence, he must become actively involved with his customers.

Steve began waiting on two customers a day and did not allow himself to hide in the back room. It wasn't long before he was thrilled with his newly-found success in helping his customers. Steve told me, "I know this sounds silly, but I never realized that the reason a customer comes into the store is to buy something and all I have to do is help them. I was always too preoccupied with doing something wrong or making a mistake. I was so afraid of failing that I didn't want to even try."

Steve didn't become a good salesperson overnight, but even his early failures were successes because they enabled him to gain experience. In very little time, what was once a terrifying fear turned into an exciting challenge that gave Steve more energy and impetus to meet each new day. The person who is reluctant to take a chance and make mistakes is bound to produce more failure. While it may sound simplistic, the old adage is true: If you don't get up to bat, how will you ever get a hit?

By doing all you can on your way to your personal peace process, you guarantee that the next time you face a fear that is keeping you from making change, you will be able to look at it confidently and work through it. You will do this because you have developed courage to face challenges head-on. You won't be overwhelmed by the fear or deny its existence. You won't worry that you will fail. You will understand that whatever happens, you have already made great strides toward your personal peace. To do this, you must send the same message to your brain again and again: The healthy thing to do is to try. It will be worth the temporary discomfort you meet when you face your fear head on. You may have to push yourself to get started since motivation is often hard to produce. Keep in mind that once you get started, you will probably be spurred on to do even more to reach your goal. Even if, despite all the courage in the world, you fail to reach your goal, you will be able to congratulate yourself for taking the first step and facing your fear of change directly.

As you experience each moment of your precious time in this world, what kind of life style makes sense to you? Intellectually and emotionally, do you agree that the most rewarding path to take in life is one that entails the courage to change? Do you agree with the premise that we must treat ourselves the very best we can? Do you think and do the things that help bring about more self-respect, intellectual stimulation, emotional excitement, career achievement, and a solid family life? If so, you are headed in the direction of becoming one of those people who perceive themselves as capable of seeking and accomplishing anything.

Happiness is out there waiting for everyone, no matter how bad things may seem at the moment. Your chances of finding it will be greatly increased if you take each opportunity that comes along to grow as a person. Striving to make good things happen should be your goal. Think and act like a strong, courageous person, and you will begin to feel and be a strong, courageous person.

As the saying goes, we usually get what we deserve. Make sure you get the best. You deserve it!

Chapter Six

IDENTIFYING AND ACKNOWLEDGING THE PROBLEM

Close to the end of World War II, one of my army assignments was to organize the construction of a displaced person's camp in Germany. The inhabitants of that camp were mostly Jews who had been released from Nazi concentration camps. They had come from the worst living conditions imaginable, and there was concern that the camp would not be kept free of disease-carrying vermin. To carry out the directive, we set up a DDT fumigation tent to delouse the camp population. But first, we had to earn the confidence of the people, all of whom knew friends and loved ones who had been tricked into thinking they were being led by the Nazis into harmless showers. And so, to gain their cooperation and trust, I explained to the former inmates exactly what we planned to do. In fact, I went through the delousing procedure myself.

As these poor souls inspected the delousing facility, I waited at the exit side of the tent, hoping to answer questions and help in any way possible. There I could gaze into their faces and wonder what could be going through their minds. What I saw astounded the imagination. Some had no legs, others no arms. One young boy used a crude stick for an artificial leg. A young woman in her early twenties approached me. She was quite beautiful, but there was a look of terror about her. I will never forget the sadness in her eyes. She was aware that our delousing project was meeting with a good deal of opposition and had decided to act as a spokesperson for the entire group.

"We appreciate what you are doing," she said. "These tents seem like palaces to us. The food, clothes, and bedding are luxuries we have not seen in a long time. Now that we understand your concern about disease spreading through the camp, we will gladly cooperate. But after all we have been through, do you think a few insects will bother us?"

The young survivor made a good point. By comparison with the life-threatening experiences they had endured, the bugs we were so concerned about must have seemed like a very minor problem to them. Perhaps the next time you are worried about a problem, you will be able to gauge its seriousness and then give it the concern it merits. Going through tough situations sometimes develops life-long strength. It's important, therefore, not to view all your problems as catastrophic. Look at them as opportunities to resolve tough situations and become stronger.

Identifying and acknowledging one's problems are the very first steps toward positive and meaningful change. In order to help you recognize where your problem areas lie, you will be guided through a self-assessment. This is a way for you to start getting to know yourself in all areas of your life. In this chapter, you will have to ask yourself some probing questions about what is bothering you and assess your symptoms. You will also get to see where your strengths lie.

The self-assessment is designed to assist you in identifying your problems and your assets to better help make the changes you desire. You may already know exactly what you want to work on, or you may have some idea of the problems, but aren't exactly sure how to pinpoint them. On the other hand, you may not even know what the problems are at all. The self-assessment will help you get to know yourself in greater depth. By the time you have completed this and the next chapter, you should have a clear vision of the areas in your life that you wish to change.

We have already seen that denial is a defense mechanism that is not helpful for people seeking their personal peace. Therefore, denying you have a problem or that your life can be enhanced in some way may be your greatest enemy during these exercises. Be as honest as possible when you answer the questions in this chapter. The only person looking at the answers will be you, so be realistic, complete, and, most important, honest.

Given that identifying and acknowledging one's problems or areas for growth are often the hardest step, you may be feeling a bit anxious and confused, while at the same time feeling very eager to face your concerns. It is important to keep your long-term goals in view. What you are about to do is akin to cleaning up an attic where papers and boxes have collected for years. Before you can file the papers and stack the boxes neatly, you must go through everything in order to determine what you want to save and what needs to be thrown away. You might start by emptying all the boxes and throwing the contents on the floor. For a while, the attic may look even messier and disorganized. But after some time, sorting through it all, everything will find its place. This is what you are about to do: throw everything on the floor in order to look at it and decide what to keep, what to throw away, and what to change. Let's get started.

Sometimes psychological problems first present themselves in the form of physical symptoms. Take a look at this concept through the experience of Lawrence.

Lawrence, a forty-three-year-old pharmacist, was suffering from frequent stomachaches. He was certain that he had developed ulcers. After a thorough physical, his doctor reassured him that no underlying medical condition was causing his physical discomfort and referred him to me for psychotherapy.

Once in therapy, Lawrence noticed that stomach pain was not his only problem. Describing himself as nearly always "tense and nervous," he pondered: "You asked what I saw as my problems. I would have to say that I could use more confidence. I don't think I stand up for myself enough. And then there's the issue of dating. Although I'm not bad looking, I always feel that attractive women will never be interested in me."

Lawrence had just identified two major problem areas in his life: health and romantic relationships. His low self-concept and feelings of anxiety were found to be a major factor in both of them.

Lawrence's presenting problem, his stomachaches, represented just the tip of the iceberg. He generally was feeling empty and unfulfilled. Had he not ultimately been debilitated by what appeared to be a medical problem, he might never have begun tackling the various interpersonal concerns that were affecting his whole life.

When looking into Lawrence's childhood, I learned his parents were not particularly mean or abusive.

He grew up in the Midwest on a farm, and his parents were simple, hard-working churchgoers. What he missed in childhood was a loving connection. His parents were often too busy to encourage him, talk to him, or even spend time with him. That is, to provide needed nurturing. As far back as he could remember, he always felt as if he had caused his parents to withdraw their emotional support. As an adult, he still considered himself unworthy of affection.

So here we see how Lawrence's childhood planted the seeds for his feeling inadequate and ill-at-ease with people.

As Lawrence went through this discovery process, he continued to hide behind idealizations of his parents. It was very hard for him to acknowledge that his parents had any connection to the way he is as an adult.

"My parents are well-intentioned, although they never read a psychology book or a book on parenting. They showed us they cared by working hard and providing a nice home and religious training. I am lucky that they let me go to a liberal arts college in the east."

It took quite a while for Lawrence to be ready to face the shortcomings in his parents. Ultimately, long-term change does require coming to terms with the source of one's problems. The farther back you can trace a negative life pattern, the greater your chance of changing it for good.

In order to begin to change, you must first face your problems. This sometimes troubling realization may take a while to sink in because it involves accepting a certain degree of uncertainty. To acknowledge that you have had a problem for years means that you can't hope to rid yourself of it overnight. Change requires patience, dedication, and sacrifice. You are embarking on a long journey, and you may experience some emotional pain and discomfort along the way. This is a normal part of the process. Nevertheless, if you do make the commitment to keep pressing forward even in trying moments, you will reach your goals.

As with Lawrence, many people starting out on their own personal peace process are not sure where they are headed. Little did he know that coming to therapy for his stomachaches would eventually lead him to better relationships with women. Now it's time for you to start learning more about yourself. Whether you know exactly what you want to change in your life or not, the exercises in this chapter will allow you to view yourself in a light that you may have never seen.

EXERCISE 6: LIFE AREAS

Consider the following life areas:

(1) Health
(2) Finances
(3) Self-Help
(4) Emotions
(5) Family
(6) Romantic Relationships

(7) Sex
(8) Religion
(9) Occupation
(10) Hobbies
(11) Other

For this exercise, write down anything that comes into your head that might be pertinent in helping you understand your thoughts and feelings regarding each area of life. (Use the chart provided on the following page.) For example, if Lawrence were doing this exercise, he might write the following:

Health:	"Stomachaches, headaches."
Finances:	"I'd like a better retirement plan."
Self-help:	"I wish I were more self-confident."
Emotions:	"I wish I could be less tense and anxious."
Family:	"I would like to start a family."
Relationships:	"I need to work on building a long-term relationship. I am afraid attractive, interesting women would never go out with me."
Sex:	"I am usually too tense to enjoy it much."
Religion:	"I have lots of guilty feelings instilled in me by my religious upbringing."
Hobbies:	"I don't have enough hobbies. I really should watch less TV and do more interesting things in my free time."
Other:	"I feel that life is passing me by."

Now on the next page, fill in the questionnaire with your own answers. Feel free to be as extensive as you'd like in filling in the form. Use extra paper if needed.

Exercise 6: Life Areas

<u>Life Areas</u>

Check off the problem area(s) that applies to you and list the associated issues in the space provided.

☐ 1. Health _____
_____

☐ 2. Finances _____
_____

☐ 3. Self-help _____
_____

☐ 4. Emotions _____
_____

☐ 5. Family _____
_____

☐ 6. Relationships _____
_____

☐ 7. Sex _____
_____

☐ 8. Religion _____
_____

☐ 9. Occupation _____
_____

☐ 10. Hobbies _____
_____

☐ 11. Other _____
_____

EXERCISE 7: SELF-IMAGE

A person's self-perception is a highly important part of one's total being. The way we see ourselves, our strengths and our weaknesses, determines, to a great extent, how we think and act. Our perceptions of our own successes are directly related to how we view ourselves.

It's important, therefore, to identify the negative labels that people frequently attach to themselves. In future chapters, your goal will be to change the negative ways in which you view yourself to a more ideal, positive self. Failure to do so will only cause emotional unrest and further feelings of low self-esteem. This conflict between your ongoing self-concept and your ideal self can be changed, but it will take some effort on your part. To continue viewing yourself as an inferior person is to deepen your feelings of anxiety and depression. This exercise presents an extensive list of personal characteristics, both positive and negative. You will be looking at each, one by one, to decide whether that characteristic describes you.

Before beginning the exercise, I want to discuss some of the most common characteristics of self-image that people identify with in terms of wanting to change. A case example illustrates each concept. In addition to characteristics that you may want to change, there are many words in the exercise that constitute strengths that you will want to be aware of to utilize later in the process.

Common characteristics that people often describe as traits they want to change:

Passivity

Laura frequently let people, such as her husband Arthur, tell her what to do. Ever since childhood, she denied her own needs in order to not "rock the boat." Rarely expressing herself, she tried as hard as she could to adapt to the whims of others. Aged forty and a mother of three, she still did not know how to assert her needs.

Laura's passivity affected all her relationships. She was unable to say no. She routinely did favors for her friends, but was reticent about requesting anything in return. She even felt embarrassed about speaking up to salespeople when she went shopping. "I can be talked into buying dresses that I don't even like!" she admitted.

Indecisiveness

Eric had difficulty making important decisions from an early age. It took him forever to finish college because he was unable to decide on a major, changing his mind countless times. He knew it was important for his future, but nonetheless became paralyzed by significant decisions, never staying with one idea for too long. He changed jobs time after time. He had few friends and had not gone out on a date for years. As a child, Eric was always told he wouldn't amount to anything. As an adult, he fulfilled that expectation. Eric was stuck believing that he was worthless. His indecisiveness stemmed from this belief. He figured, why should he decide on anything if he was moving without much purpose or direction?

Jealousy

Jerry's jealousy was driving his wife Melissa away. Only a few weeks after they got married, he displayed a side that Melissa had never seen. She started to feel as if she were his employee, not his wife. Jerry sought to determine where she could go, who she could spend time with, and for how long. He also strictly controlled the couple's finances giving Melissa only the bare minimum to cover the household costs. Jerry's controlling behavior was motivated by deep feelings of insecurity. On some level, he was convinced that Melissa would leave him for another man.

Guilt

Dan is filled with guilt. "I have failed my children," he asserts. Having divorced his wife years earlier, he didn't hold up his end of the child support settlement. At that time in his life, he was irresponsible. Dan was in his early twenties at the time and had a great deal of growing to do. Now in his late thirties, he feels a great deal of guilt for not having kept in contact with his children and not supporting them on any level as he feels he should have. "I am a lousy father and a pretty rotten person, too."

Negativity

Mitchell's negative thinking is leading him to give up hope. "I am forty-six, and if I didn't meet the 'right woman' at thirty-two, how is it going to happen now? All my friends are married. I know deep down that there is something wrong with me. It's not worth even going out on dates anymore. Even if I did have a date, she would dump me as soon as she found out that I don't have a high paying job or a nice car. I am such a loser."

Inferiority

A bright woman, Kathleen limits her options by not giving herself enough credit. Even though she was a straight-A student during college, she dropped out right before her senior year to get married. Now she works in an unfulfilling job and doesn't envision doing anything else. "I know my husband wants me to go back to college, but it seems like such a chore. I have been out of school for so long, I'm sure I wouldn't be able to keep up. All of those young kids would be much ahead of me. I also don't think that I am smart enough to get through the coursework."

Depression

Lois often feels that she is on the verge of tears. She has trouble concentrating when people are speaking to her. Her husband often puts her down, and she hates her dead-end job. Missing many days from work, Lois feels that she just cannot drag herself out of bed. She finds herself taking out her frustration on her four children. "Everything is coming down on me. Sometimes I feel that life is just not worth living."

The above illustrations are a clear understanding of how a person's self-perceptions affect one's whole life. It can affect it negatively, as seen in the above examples. Or it can be just the opposite: your self-perceptions can affect your life in a positive manner, as long as they are positive self-perceptions. By completing the following exercise, you will get to see which characteristics you believe describe you best. Go through the list, slowly and carefully, checking off the words that you feel describe characteristics of your personality.

Exercise 7: Self-Image

Check the words that describe yourself. You may notice that there are some words that fall into both the positive and the negative columns. Aggressive, for example, falls into both. Someone can be aggressive in a positive way, like going after that great job opportunity, while others can be too aggressive, pushing people around in a negative way. In cases like this, check off the word in the column that fits how you believe this characteristic works for you—positively or negatively.

POSITIVE CHARACTERISTICS	NEGATIVE CHARACTERISTICS
O Aggressive	O Absent-minded
O Alert	O Afraid
O Assertive	O Aggravated
O Attentive	O Aggressive
O Attractive	O Agitated
O Bold	O Angry
O Brave	O Anxious
O Brilliant	O Apathetic
O Calm	O Apprehensive
O Capable	O Argumentative
O Cautious	O Belligerent
O Cheerful	O Bold
O Clever	O Bored
O Competent	O Bossy
O Confident	O Cautious
O Considerate	O Compulsive
O Courageous	O Confused
O Creative	O Constricted
O Daring	O Controlled

O	Defensive	O	Cowardly
O	Demanding	O	Cynical
O	Dependable	O	Daring
O	Efficient	O	Defensive
O	Elated	O	Demanding
O	Energetic	O	Dependent
O	Enthusiastic	O	Depressed
O	Excited	O	Despondent
O	Forgiving	O	Devastated
O	Friendly	O	Disgusted
O	Generous	O	Distracted
O	Gentle	O	Disturbed
O	Gregarious	O	Embarrassed
O	Happy	O	Envious
O	Honest	O	Fearful
O	Hopeful	O	Foolish
O	Humorous	O	Forgetful
O	Imaginative	O	Fragile
O	Independent	O	Frustrated
O	Intelligent	O	Guilty
O	Interesting	O	Helpless
O	Inventive	O	Hostile
O	Jovial	O	Immature
O	Level headed	O	Impatient
O	Likeable	O	Impractical
O	Logical	O	Inadequate
O	Loving	O	Incompetent
O	Moral	O	Indifferent
O	Motivated	O	Inferior
O	Neat	O	Inhibited
O	Non-conforming	O	Irrational
O	Opinionated	O	Irritable
O	Optimistic	O	Lazy

O	Original	O	Listless
O	Patient	O	Lonely
O	Pensive	O	Manipulative
O	Philosophical	O	Mean
O	Poised	O	Misunderstood
O	Polite	O	Monotonous
O	Practical	O	Morbid
O	Productive	O	Negative
O	Rational	O	Non-conforming
O	Relaxed	O	Obnoxious
O	Reserved	O	Opinionated
O	Resilient	O	Passive
O	Respectful	O	Pessimistic
O	Responsible	O	Preoccupied
O	Romantic	O	Rejected
O	Self-centered	O	Reserved
O	Self-reliant	O	Restless
O	Sensitive	O	Rigid
O	Sexy/Sexual	O	Rude
O	Sincere	O	Sad
O	Sociable	O	Scared
O	Suspicious	O	Self-centered
O	Sympathetic	O	Self-destructive
O	Tolerant	O	Shy
O	Trustworthy	O	Sinful
O	Unconventional	O	Stupid
O	Unpredictable	O	Suicidal
O	Wise	O	Suspicious
O	Worthwhile	O	Tense
		O	Tired
		O	Ugly
		O	Unassertive

	O Uncomfortable
	O Unconventional
	O Unfriendly
	O Unpredictable
	O Unreasonable
	O Weak
	O Worried
	O Worthless

Look over the words that you have checked. Do you feel that they give a realistic and accurate description of who you are? Can you readily see your strengths? Can you readily see the areas you'd most like to change? Did you learn anything new about yourself from this exercise?

PUTTING IT ALL TOGETHER

Good work! You have done a great deal toward identifying and acknowledging your problem areas and characteristics, as well as identifying your strengths. By completing the exercises in this chapter, you have hopefully gotten to know yourself better. You may have found that there are one or two areas that cause you difficulty in your life that you are choosing to change. Or you may have found a great many. You are going to need to narrow down your focus to one or two areas that you really want to tackle. Your chance of long-term success is greatly increased if you don't overwhelm yourself, especially at first, with too many goals. Often just bringing a problem to awareness is enough for a person to be on alert for this trait, and steer clear of it when it appears. So don't worry if all your goals are not attended to right away. After you reach your initial goals to satisfaction, you can review your responses to these exercises again and create new ones.

On the next page I want you to summarize what you have learned about yourself from this chapter. Fill in between one and three of the most important issues from Exercise 6, Life Areas, that you would like to work on, then do the same for Exercise 7, Self-Image. This summary page will help you focus as you move on to create goals in later chapters. Looking at your summary page, you should feel very proud of how hard you have worked and how much you have learned about yourself since you began the process.

IDENTIFY AND ACKNOWLEDGE YOUR PROBLEMS

SUMMARY PAGE

Exercise 6–Life Areas:

1)_____

2)_____

3)_____
Additional Comments:

_____

_____

_____

Exercise 7–Self-Image:

1)_____

2)_____

3)_____

Additional Comments:

_____

_____

_____

PART THREE

YOUR PERSONAL PEACE PROCESS

Chapter Seven

THE PEACE PLAN

In the preceding sections, you have taken a "self-inventory." You have explored your problem areas, logged your symptoms, begun to explore your childhood, assessed your hopefulness for change, identified your coping styles, begun to monitor your thinking patterns, and learned some new tools to help you on your journey. Now you are ready to focus on your destination—your personal peace process. The first step in this process is establishing a realistic plan of action, which we will call the *peace plan*.

Go back and review the life areas and associated issues that you have identified in Exercise 6 in chapter six. Now copy the problems to the chart on the following page (Exercise 8), numbering all the items in terms of rank, placing "1" next to the easiest one to tackle, "2" next to the next easiest, and so on. In addition, place an asterisk next to any symptom or problem that must be addressed right away (e.g., Lawrence's stomachaches).

You should be able to use your numbered list to think about specific goals and priorities that you want to set. In general, try to concentrate on no more than one symptom or problem area at a time. Start at the top of your list (with the easiest issues) and move on down, unless you have a pressing problem (one that you asterisked). Tackling the easiest issues first will likely give you satisfaction and the confidence to keep moving forward. If you try to begin with the toughest issues first, you may wind up sabotaging your efforts and giving up.

Exercise 8: Problem list

Problem   *Rank.*

_____   _____
_____   _____
_____   _____
_____   _____
_____   _____
_____   _____
_____   _____

Perhaps, like Lawrence, you have identified several major changes that you would like to make. Though Lawrence's stated problem was his health (i.e., his stomachaches), he was contemplating a career move and also looking to date more. Furthermore, he suffered from the core issue of poor self-esteem. This exercise is meant not to dictate any specific course of action, but simply to help you formulate your options in order to establish a plan of action. Lawrence decided first to concentrate on his health along with his lack of self-esteem. He thought he would focus on dating as soon as he felt better. Further down the road, he might consider other challenges and goals, such as continuing his education in order to get more out of his career.

Now it's your turn. Over the course of this book, you have given much thought to the sources of your frustrations in the past and present. Now it's time to shift gears and start building your future by planning a course of action. In order to develop a realistic game-plan, you will need to review the list you just made and pick out the first few problems you wish to work on. You are going to start your goal worksheet (Exercise 9 on the following page) with these initial problems. In addition to including specific problems from your problem list on your goal worksheet, include any personal traits you want to change from Exercise 7 (Self-Image) in Chapter 6.

So, you have identified the problem; now, what would you like the end result to be? This may take some careful consideration. In the "Vision" column next to the problem area on the goal worksheet, list your ideas of the results you would like to see. Your vision of your goals can be as small or as vast as you want it to be. Your goals can be anything from cutting down your gum chewing or stopping smoking to getting out of an unsatisfying or abusive relationship or becoming an independent businessperson. Let's say that you listed finances as a problem area;

be specific about how you would like to improve your situation. Would you like to be independently wealthy, or do you simply want more pocket money? Either goal is perfectly reasonable; you just need to decide for yourself what is best suited to your needs and desires.

Now that you've identified the vision you see for each problem, you need to break down your work into manageable chunks. Your goal worksheet is divided into the following categories: short-term goals (within one month), medium-term goals (within three months), and long-term goals (over three months). A long-term goal might be finding a new job or starting a new relationship. In contrast, improving communication with your current partner might fall into the short-term category.

Exercise 9: Goal Worksheet

For each of the applicable problems you listed from the previous chapters, list your short-term, medium–term, and long-term goals. Start with the top priorities from your Problem List at the beginning of this chapter. If you need more space, continue on a separate sheet of paper.

Problem	*Vision*	*Short Term Goals* (within 1 month)	*Med. Term Goals* (1-3 months)	*Long Term Goals* (over 3 months)
#1.				
#2.				

#3.				

Peter, a forty-year-old salesman, was married and had two sons. He came to therapy because he was depressed. He considered himself a failure. Although he had gone to a prominent business school, he was not able to land a job in management. His home life was also stressful. He and his wife could not cope with conflicts and sometimes would go a day or two without speaking to one another. He also felt guilty because he found himself snapping at his children on a regular basis.

On his problem-areas exercise from Chapter 6, Peter had checked off the following life areas: finances, self-help, emotions, family, relationships, occupation, and hobbies. Through his self-image exercises, he also determined that he felt guilt, engaged in negative thinking, suffered from poor self-esteem, lacked initiative, and had difficulty managing his anger. Peter also discovered that he was a very passive man. He rarely expressed his anger and frustration even when others were rude to him. For example, he didn't say anything when a coworker repeatedly made fun of his foreign sounding last name.

Peter's goal worksheet looked like the one on the following page:

Peter's Goal Worksheet

Problem	Vision	Short Term Goals (within 1 month)	Med. Term Goals (1-3 months)	Long Term Goals (over 3 months)
1. Poor Family Relationships	To have a satisfying relationship with my wife and sons	• Make a weekly date with my wife to do something that we both enjoy • Help my sons with their homework two nights a week • Set aside Sunday mornings to do something fun with my family	• Improve communication with my wife by setting aside time to talk with each other about our relationship, assess what our problems are together, and try to listen to each other's point of view without becoming defensive	• Feel more confident and satisfied with the direction that my relationships are taking • Talk to the children and note how they feel about our family and the changes we've made • Be open to modifications based on the discussions we have as a family, taking everyone's feelings into consideration and not getting defensive

2. I am not assertive and I let people take advantage of me at work	To be more assertive and self-assured at work, and to feel entitled to be treated with respect	• Confront my coworker about his jokes about my name, letting him know that I don't find them funny. In fact, I find them offensive and it makes me angry. I am entitled to be angry and am justified in protecting myself	• Ask my employer for a detailed assessment of my job performance. • Assess his responses and try to make the changes that seem appropriate	• Decide if this is a job that I want to remain with • If it still proves to be unsatisfying, make the steps to find another job in which I'd feel challenged and enriched
3. I have feelings of anxiety and depression	To rid myself of these feelings and replace them with peace of mind	• Begin to make sense of my feelings • Begin a journal and keep a log of when these feelings arise, how long they last, and what precipitates them	• Continue my journal and start to see if any patterns are apparent as to when and why these feelings occur • Start to write in my journal about my childhood experiences of feeling depressed and anxious • Try to uncover the sources of my feelings	• Continue the journal and look for patterns that are not in my best interest • Continue writing about my childhood in order to understand the factors that influenced my life • If I am not feeling better, I will seek professional help

Over the course of several months, Peter identified the roots of his problems through journal writing, talking with his wife, and psychotherapy. Peter told me, "My childhood, to put it mildly, wasn't ideal. My parents came from Czechoslovakia. They did all right considering the adjustment problems they had with immigrating. However, I missed a lot growing up compared to what typical American kids had. My parents were too preoccupied with just getting by and making ends meet. They had little time to concern themselves with the emotional welfare of my siblings and me."

Peter realized that his childhood had led to a weak self-concept that would not go away overnight. At the same time, he also understood that he could start experimenting with new kinds of behaviors right away. He thus decided to confront his co-worker who would kid him about his last name and call him "the Czech."

For months, Peter had seethed in silence about his coworker's remarks. Although his heart was pounding, he expressed his displeasure and asked his coworker to stop. To Peter's surprise, his coworker said, "Okay. I never knew you didn't find it funny because you always seemed to laugh too! I'll stop."

Peter had never realized his silence was contributing to the problem. He had been laughing because he feared his coworker would know that he was actually angry. He was sending the coworker a false message. Now that they were both honest about the situation, the problem was resolved.

Peter's peace plan illustrates how you can make headway on reducing your symptoms and giving up your self-defeating behaviors. You may have noticed in Peter's goal worksheet that, in articulating some of his goals, he employed some very positive and healthy thinking and behavior. Think about some of the resistance tools you read about in chapter four. Peter structured his goals to attack his issues head-on and as a strong, courageous person, avoiding utilizing defense mechanisms and negative thinking that so often held him back before. Perhaps without realizing it, Peter employed three very important principles of change:

PRINCIPLES OF CHANGE

Principle #1: TREAT YOURSELF WITH RESPECT AND CARE

Principle #2: FACE PROBLEMS AND CONFLICTS DIRECTLY

Principle #3: IDENTIFY, UNDERSTAND, AND LET GO OF RESISTANCES

These principles are simply incompatible with unhealthy thinking. Each time you act according to these principles, you are redefining yourself and becoming a stronger person. As Peter realized, it does take time to reverse a weak self-concept. However, as you slowly begin to handle situations in healthier ways, you will automatically find yourself feeling and being stronger, more self-confident, and able to take on what used to seem like big problems.

"OKAY, I'VE GOT THE PLAN, BUT HOW LONG WILL IT TAKE?"

As people seek to reduce their problems and pursue long-term goals, they often ask how long the changes will take. There is not a ready answer because so many factors come into play. In general, the longer your problems have existed and the more severe they are, the longer they take to change. For example, if you noted particularly traumatic experiences on your childhood misfortune checklist from chapter three, such as abuse by a parent, change is likely to take more time because of the complexity of the emotions involved. A review of your present coping styles will enable you to determine their effectiveness. If you have been sidestepping your problems and using defenses such as "avoidance" and "projection/blame," you may not be able to develop more effective ones right away. Likewise, if you notice that you are troubled by particularly disturbing thoughts, you may need to work hard in order to change your thinking.

Wherever you are starting from, it is crucial that you not be self-critical. Be sure not to blame yourself for how you have learned to cope with your problems until now. Wherever you are starting from, it is important to be accepting of yourself. It is also very important not to blame or abuse yourself with negative thoughts about your progress in attaining your goals.

Remember Principle #1, treat yourself with respect and care.

IT'S THE DIRECTION THAT COUNTS

Once you establish your peace plan, you may find yourself proceeding faster, or slower, than you had expected.

Bill entered therapy after a serious auto accident. An auto parts salesman, Bill had begun to fear driving and no longer could drive to his customers located throughout New York and New Jersey.

Bill and I developed a peace plan designed to help him overcome his fear of driving. His first assignment was to sit in his car as it was parked in the driveway. Next, he had to sit in it and turn on the ignition. His next assignment was to drive around his block. When he was comfortable with this, he was to drive around his town. Finally after progressing for about four months, he felt ready to meet his biggest challenge, highway driving. I encouraged him to drive for ten minutes on the highway and then stop in a rest area and sit in his car for ten minutes at a rest stop. If he felt okay, he was to drive for ten more minutes, rest, and then for ten more. After the second break, he found that he no longer needed to stop and he drove all the way to his customer.

Each situation is unique. If Bill had returned home after his first ten minutes, that would have been fine. He still would have been making progress toward his goal. Your own personal peace process may need to come in small steps, but as long as you are making progress in the right direction, you will continue to feel better and better.

BE REALISTIC

Finally, we all need to dream, but at the same time we must be realistic. To wish for the unattainable is to set ourselves up for failure. Many years ago, I met the famous singer, Roland Hayes. He told me about a young lady who came to him one day claiming she'd been praying, saving, and planning for the day when she could study with the great Mr. Hayes. Sadly, the young woman had no talent at all, Hayes recalled. "With all her wishing," he told me, "she forgot to pray for a voice."

That doesn't mean you should stop trying to reach your goals. It does mean you must be realistic about them. As Robert Browning once reminded us all, "Ah, but a man's reach should exceed his grasp, or what's a heaven for?" The point is, reach high, but don't set yourself up for failure by reaching for what is not possible.

Chapter Eight

PUTTING YOUR PLAN INTO ACTION

For any activity I can think of, whether it is sports, business, dieting, war, traveling, or whatever, the best plan is worthless if it is not executed well. Think about sports. What happens when your favorite basketball team is down by two points and they have just recovered the ball with nine seconds left in the game? A timeout is called and the coach devises a strategic play that eats up the clock, leaving just enough time for the star shooter to get the ball just behind the three-point line and take the final, winning shot of the game. There may be fakes, picks, screens, and passes included in this plan designed to completely throw the defense off so that the shooter is left completely open to take that last shot. This may be the best nine-second offensive plan ever devised. This coach may consistently come up with the best play plans in all of basketball. But how many times have you seen the ball get put back into play, the clock start ticking down (nine-eight-seven), the dribbler looking for an open pass (six-five), the shooter trying to shake his defender (four-three), the passer seeing the open shooter (two-one), passing the ball, and the shooter getting the final shot off (zero) just after the buzzer sounds, a split second too late. Game over. The perfect plan was worthless, since it was not well-executed.

In most situations in life, you need a sound plan and a strong execution in order to be successful. I am often asked which is more important, a good plan or good execution. I have always said that both are important. A good plan, like the basketball coach's, was unsuccessful because it was not executed well—the players took too long and the clock ran out. On the other hand, you could have a team of very strong executors, like the construction workers digging the channel tunnel (the Chunnel) between England and France, one group starting from Calais, France and the other starting from Folkestone, England, both with the goal of meeting to complete the project in the middle of the English Channel, fifty miles offshore. These skilled workers and technicians could be doing the best drilling, excavating, and digging work in all of Europe. They could be the fastest, the safest, the most economical, and the highest quality construction workers on the continent. However, if the engineering plans had not been good, not accurate, or not complete, this outstanding execution would not have led to success. In fact, poor plans in this case could easily have led to cost overruns, schedule delays, and very likely ruined careers.

Success requires sound planning and effective execution. You have just created your personal peace plan. So how do you ensure sound execution? How do you get started?

If you've ever gone to the beach and wanted to go swimming when the water is particularly cold, you probably did one of two things:

(1) You stood at the edge of the shore for a while, letting the cold water run up over your feet several times as the tide brought it in and out, then slowly, you waded in a bit further so the water did not come up past your knees and you stood there until the chilling cold feeling did not feel quite that painful. Then, again slowly, you may have gone in up to your waist, waiting again before going any further. You may have continued this process until you finally found yourself in the water up to your chin, at which time, the water was much less biting and much more refreshing, since you were used to it after the ten minutes it took you to get submerged.

(2) You may have simply stood on the sand, began running toward the water, crossed over the edge of the sea, and as soon as you were deep enough to dive without hitting bottom, you plunged your entire body in, head-first.

Either way, you ended up in the sea, swimming. One way took longer, but both were effective. Both got you into the water in a way in which you were comfortable. Beginning to put your peace plan into action is not entirely different.

Depending on whether you are a person who likes to plunge into the water head-first or take more deliberate, slower steps to get used to it before getting too wet, you may want to try different approaches to getting started on your plan. For those who need help getting started, or who are more comfortable taking it a bit slower, I recommend that you start by making a promise.

MAKE A PROMISE AND KEEP IT

First, make a promise to yourself that you are going to begin working on your peace plan. Since this book has taught you that you must treat yourself with respect, and you know that breaking a promise you've made to yourself would be disrespectful, you should be able to keep that promise and begin executing your plan.

But what if that doesn't work? What if your promise to yourself is not strong enough? What if you keep finding excuses to avoid putting your plan into action? What if other priorities keep getting in the way?

The second part of the promise is actually making the promise to someone else. Find a close friend or a relative, someone you trust, and make a commitment to them. Share your goals with them and your plan for achieving your goals. Commit to them that you will begin to work toward those goals and that you would like to provide them progress reports every week, or at every milestone. Ask your friend to check in with you periodically, to make sure that you are meeting your commitments to yourself and to them. Most people who really want to change, even though they may have trouble keeping commitments they make to themselves, will want to try very hard to keep commitments they make to others. This is particularly true for people who have come as far as putting together their personal peace plan. We don't like to let other people down, even if we are experts at letting ourselves down.

BREAK IT INTO SMALLER CHUNKS

Having made a promise to yourself and perhaps a trusted friend, your goal achievement still may seem overwhelming to you. The good news is there is a relatively simple way to make your goals seem much less overwhelming. Have you ever met one of those people who seem to have the confidence to do anything? Nothing seems too hard, too much, too big to them. They seem to be able to take on any task or challenge with the attitude that they can do it. The reality is these people are not looking at the specific challenge as one big, overwhelming task. Rather, they are looking at it as dozens of small, very doable tasks. It's often as simple as that—breaking down your task or goal into smaller, more manageable chunks. This way, no one chunk seems too big or too overwhelming to attack. Aside from allowing you to see your plan as a much more manageable set of tasks, the additional benefit is that you begin to get some early wins, and you begin to build up momentum. Successfully knocking off a few smaller tasks in the initial days or weeks of executing your plan will give you a boost of confidence, a taste of success, and the momentum and enthusiasm to continue winning. Success breeds success. Momentum is a powerful and wonderful thing.

As you organize your specific goals into smaller, more manageable pieces, think about what prerequisites or requirements you will need to help you. These requirements could come in several forms. You may need help from specific people, you may need money to fund parts of your plan, you may need certain information, or you may simply need time. The more you can identify your resource requirements upfront, the better off and less disappointed you will be once you are deep into your execution and you find you need to find some people or some money that you had not identified before.

VISUALIZING SUCCESS

One of the most successful techniques I've used with some of my patients is called *visualization*. This is a technique where you imagine yourself successfully completing your goals or enjoying positive situations, thanks to having achieved your goals. Visualization can be used for many advantages. One use of visualization is for people who have self-esteem issues. By visualizing themselves as strong, confident, proud, talented, valuable individuals, they can overcome the poor self-image they have programmed themselves into believing. Visualization can be a very powerful tool for seeing yourself in a different, more positive light.

In the case of getting started on executing your plan, visualization is also helpful. You can visualize yourself crossing the finish line of that bike race you have been too nervous to enter, or you can visualize yourself having dinner and conversation with that woman whom you see on the train every morning but are too shy to ask out. After being able to visualize yourself in these positive situations, actually getting started in making the first moves is much easier. Here's how to do it:

Visualization works best when you are deeply relaxed. Find a way to get yourself in a state of deep relaxation. Lying in bed at night right before falling asleep or in the morning just after waking up are two great times for practicing and using visualization. Your body and your mind are usually at a very relaxed state then. You can practice visualization at any other time during the day as well, as long as you are able to completely relax and tune out all other distractions. If you've ever done meditation, this is similar. You want to create a state where there is no tension whatsoever in your body. Your feet, legs, arms, neck, jaw, eyes, back, and mind are comfortable, relaxed, and practically floating.

Once you are in your relaxed, undistracted state, let yourself create scenes in your mind where you are working toward and achieving your goals. Create realistic scenes. If your goal is to enter and complete the local bike race coming up this summer, you may not want to start by visualizing yourself passing Lance Armstrong on the Champs Elysees to win the Tour De France. It is best to imagine yourself in scenes that are more realistic, more achievable, such as crossing the finish line and receiving a finisher's medal.

Let's go back to Peter's goals from his goal worksheet in chapter seven. One of his short-term goals was to set aside Sunday mornings for fun family activities. Peter used visualization to help himself get started on his goals. He got himself into a completely relaxed state, closed his eyes, and saw his family packing the car to go to the beach. He pictured all the details: the kids putting their favorite beach toys in their bags, his wife stuffing a handful of towels into the trunk, he spreading the peanut butter and jelly onto the bread and putting sandwiches into his red cooler. He continued the visualization, driving to the shore, talking about various topics in the car with his family. He saw his boys laughing and playing in the sand, scampering into the water and running back up, shivering, to his wife for a towel. Peter saw in this visualization his family together, happy and enjoying themselves and each other. This technique made it much easier for Peter to plan and organize his family's first outing.

Other things you can do with visualization are to create the scenes in your mind of successful situations, but then toss in a roadblock or two. This enables you to anticipate potential issues and to visualize how to go about dealing with them in advance, so that if and when things do get off track, you have already thought through (and visualized) some solutions. For example, Peter may have envisioned getting ready to go to the beach when, all of a sudden, he sees the skies open up and it begins to rain. After visualizing talking it over with his wife and kids, they decide that instead of staying home and being disappointed about not being able to go to the beach, they would go roller skating as a family, or to the movies, or a museum, or some other family activity. These visualization techniques will help see that most obstacles are not big problems and can be dealt with effectively.

So whether you can jump right in and begin working on your goals, whether you need to enlist a friend to help you keep your commitment, or whether you need to do visualization exercises in order to see yourself successfully achieving your goals, start putting your plan into action today. The longer you wait after creating your peace plan before putting it into action, the higher the chance of you never putting it into action. Perhaps the most important thing you can do after creating your plan is to begin executing it right away. Because once you begin, you will succeed in some small, early pieces, fueling your confidence and building momentum to continue achieving your bigger-and longer-term goals.

Chapter Nine

AVOIDING PLAN DEVIATIONS

Change is never a straightforward process. As you move forward, you will constantly encounter pitfalls and roadblocks. What you need to do is to recognize them so they can be avoided. If you do find yourself getting sidetracked from time to time, try to be patient with yourself. It happens to everyone. I have found that many people suffer from one or many of the following plan deviations:

Deviation #1: Magical thinking

Deviation #2: Expecting a "quick fix"

Deviation #3: Impulsive behavior

Deviation #4: Going for too much, too soon

Deviation #5: Doing nothing

Deviation #6: Sabotaging oneself

Deviation #7: Waiting for a crisis

DEVIATION #1: MAGICAL THINKING

Unfortunately, change rarely happens all of a sudden. It is magical thinking to expect change overnight—worthwhile progress does take time. Nevertheless, some people still believe in magic, pretending that their problems are not real or will disappear of their own accord. I caution you not to interpret the word

89

"secrets" in the title of this book to imply there is a magical way to understand or resolve difficulties.

> George always had fantasies centered on being rich and famous. Money and possessions occupied his mind constantly. He began his career by purchasing a restaurant to operate. In the beginning, business was good, and George found himself making a very comfortable living. He purchased an expensive car, put a down payment on a beach house, and took out a large loan to open two additional restaurants. He was so eager to expand and make more money, he did not consider all the ramifications of operating three restaurants. He had problems with his personnel. He had problems paying his loans. He found he had no time for anything or anyone outside of work. He kept thinking that somehow things would straighten themselves out, but they never did.

In his search for fame and fortune, George had planted more trees than he could water. He thought getting rich would be easy, and that being rich would bring him happiness. That is magical thinking.

Such unrealistic thinking may mask deeper problems. People who feel desperate may need to comfort themselves by entering into a fantasy world. George had some deep-rooted feelings of inadequacy. Being wealthy and having expensive possessions was George's way of making himself feel more secure. Unfortunately, his magical thinking caused him to be impulsive and to not plan realistically. Despite its apparent attractions, magical thinking can get you into trouble. Use your intellect to your best advantage. Deal with the realities of what exists.

DEVIATION #2: EXPECTING A "QUICK FIX"

The personal peace process does not contain any shortcuts. If you think that you have found a rapid solution for a longstanding problem, you are probably fooling yourself. In all likelihood, you will end up wasting your time because you will need to start all over again with additional complications.

> As a house painter, Spencer was earning a comfortable living working for a contractor. After several years, he decided that he could do better working for himself. He bought some supplies and business cards. He placed the cards under the doors of all the apartments in

his neighborhood and waited for the phone to ring. It didn't. After a
few weeks, Spencer began to regret his decision.

Spencer's decision to try to "move up" was not unsound. His plan was not
even that bad. It was his expectations that were unrealistic. He didn't realize that
starting a small business was a major undertaking and that, under the best of circumstances, he might not experience much success right away. He was involved
in building something from scratch, and he needed to develop a long-term game-
plan. He also failed to anticipate that he would have to exert himself more in
order to set things in motion.

DEVIATION #3: IMPULSIVE BEHAVIOR

Change requires that you spend some time sorting out your life. If you act
before you have done your homework, you might simply create new problems.
"Think twice, work once."

A widower, Abe wanted to start dating again. Through a book club,
he started corresponding with a divorced woman in California who
shared many of his interests. Soon he flew out to meet her. A few
weeks later, he impulsively sold his house back east to marry her.

After a few short months of marriage Abe realized that he had not really found
the relationship he was seeking. His wife was involved in a demanding career and
he did not get along with her children. His impulsiveness left him worse off than
he originally had been.

DEVIATION #4: GOING FOR TOO MUCH, TOO SOON

Sometimes, people push themselves too hard once they define their specific
goals for change. They have little difficulty getting started, but end up complicat-
ing matters by being impatient and trying too hard. The truth is, sometimes the
slower you go, the faster you get there.

At fifty-five and in poor health, Gary realized he had to follow his
doctor's orders to stop smoking and lose weight. He immediately

signed up at a local health club and began working out daily. Eager to slim down as fast as possible, Gary was not satisfied with the exercise regimen suggested by his instructor. He decided to double the amount of weight that he was bench-pressing. A few days later, he injured his shoulder and was sidelined for several weeks.

Be sure to pace yourself. In many cases, your personal peace process is like running a marathon, and you can ill-afford to wear yourself out in the beginning of the race.

DEVIATION #5: DOING NOTHING

Some people who resist change find comfort in the false notion that their problems can wait.

Like Gary, Mark needed to quit smoking and lose weight. Rather than plunging headfirst into change, he erred by assuming that he had all the time in the world.

Nearing retirement from a long and successful career as an engineer, he planned to take better care of himself once he bought a boat and moved to the shore.

A devoted husband and father of two college-age children, Mark enjoyed spending time with his family. He had many hobbies, and loved to read and travel. He wasn't bothered by his bad habits. "Eating fatty foods and smoking give me great pleasure. It's simply a trade-off between being a bit out of shape and doing some things that I really enjoy." Mark died of a heart attack before he ever received his first pension check.

Sometimes change really is a matter of life and death.

DEVIATION #6: SABOTAGING ONESELF

As mentioned earlier, many people seeking change have grown up in families where they lacked love and support. As a result, they have never learned how to take proper care of themselves. Paradoxically, they may feel anxious about meeting their own needs. Change requires that you begin to treat yourself with respect.

Sarah's parents were difficult to please. No matter what she did, they criticized her. Married with two children, she entered therapy in her late thirties. Sarah had gone to college, but was stuck in a dead-end job. She dreamed of going back to school in order to launch a career in business, but was afraid of making any demands on her family.

Sarah felt depressed and angry. She would race home from her job to cook and do all the household chores. Although she felt frustrated about her daily routine, she preferred not to take any decisive action. Instead, she kept chastising herself about being a lousy wife and mother.

"My husband is a saint to put up with me. I am not the neatest person, and my cooking leaves a lot to be desired," she said. After further exploration with Sarah, she admitted that she often either burned the dinner or messed up the recipe, resulting in the meal being either sub-par or ruined.

In fact, by punishing herself, Sarah was adding to her own unhappiness. Unlike her parents, her husband did care about her welfare and did not expect her to put aside her own concerns. Unfortunately, she felt unworthy of enjoying life more.

DEVIATION #7: WAITING FOR A CRISIS

Many people feel that they must face a crisis before considering change. If your car's engine didn't sound right, you probably wouldn't hesitate to bring it to the attention of a mechanic right away. Likewise, the sooner you address personal problems, the easier it is to resolve them.

Scott waited too long to seek therapy. By the time he acknowledged his gambling problem, it had nearly ruined him. Married with two children, Scott found himself in debt. When family and friends asked him to invest their money, he couldn't resist the temptation to use it to gamble: "Initially, I had every intention of investing the money. I did feel, however, that I would win big, and would pay it back. I gambled for big stakes, and did win every once in a while. However, I should have come for help long ago. I have a sickness. I know that now."

Scott had now dug himself into a much deeper hole than mere debt. Several friends and family members were threatening to sue him, and his marriage was falling apart.

You should begin to see the advantages of making sense of your thinking and behavior, and how to recognize common plan deviations. By knowing what to look for, you can try to avoid the usual traps and stay on course within your peace plan.

Even if you do find yourself confronted with a deviation or a block, the key is not to give up. If you hit a block, you need to identify and acknowledge the block. Then determine how to get around it. If you have gotten through these past two chapters, you are off to a great start. You should be very proud of yourself for getting this far. You have already come a long way in the process. As you read on, you will see how to take your personal peace plan and put it into action, and as you begin to see the positive changes you are seeking, to make them permanent, so that negative messages and defense mechanisms do not creep back into your thinking and behavior.

Chapter Ten

CONFRONTING YOUR FEELINGS

When you engage in the kind of important personal work that you are doing right now, the task of identifying your problems, uncovering their origins, defining your goals, and beginning to implement them (in effect, changing your life), an array of feelings will undoubtedly surface. Being aware of your feelings is good; feelings deserve our attention and respect. They help us communicate with others and they help us to understand ourselves.

During your personal peace process, you may experience any combination of anger, fear, anxiety, sadness, loss and grief, hurt, rejection, guilt, as well as excitement, joy, elation, relief, love, peace, contentment, and any and every other emotion. When you are making essential life changes, you may even feel many of these emotions at the same time. Each life issue may bring up different feelings. Some feelings will be much stronger than others. However, you can't escape feelings if you want to make permanent changes.

Do not be afraid of your feelings. Many self-defeating thoughts and behavior patterns arise out of fear in order to help protect us from experiencing painful feelings. Often, feelings that upset you are an indication that you are on the right track toward healing your past wounds and present-life problems. Think of every one of your feelings as a gift that informs you about your past and present difficulties, that allows you to understand yourself better, heal, and move ahead.

Luke had a problem with being compulsive. He was forever counting things. He counted the steps it took him to walk from his home to his car and from his car to his desk at work. He counted the tiles in the kitchen floor over and over again, he counted the times the merry-go-round turned as his child rode it.

This compulsive behavior interfered significantly with Luke's life. His attention and concentration were affected because of this pre-

occupation. Once he started to do the work of reducing his counting, he found himself experiencing feelings of anger and grief that he
couldn't explain and did not want to feel. When he brought these feelings to me in therapy, we discussed how Luke's counting originated.
We were doing the work of uncovering the source of his problems.

He told me that he was terrified as a young child of his parent's
violent relationship. They would scream, throw things, and sometimes shove and hit each other. His parents did not console him and
only chastised him for showing any emotion. During their fights, the
only way Luke could keep himself calm and not experience his deep
feelings of terror and rage was to begin to count things. It got his
mind onto something else so he didn't have to focus on their fighting
and his terror. He would count everything in his bedroom until the
fight was over and he felt safe.

This behavior continued through the years, and generalized to most of Luke's
life. As Luke began to understand how his counting began, and how he used it to
protect himself from these feelings, he had a new-found respect for his ability to
cope as a child. He also realized that as an adult, this was maladaptive and damaging to his life.

Luke's feelings of anger and grief were uncovered because, in working toward
reducing his counting, these emotions had to surface. The counting always kept
the feelings down, but now Luke was getting a chance to feel what lay under his
counting. He came into my office one day in a panic because of these feelings. He
thought something was terribly wrong with the treatment and he wanted to give
up. I explained to him that his feelings were necessary in order for him to heal
his past and change his life. Luke began to work through this past trauma, and
understand that the feelings he was experiencing were the feelings of the child,
not the adult. But he also realized that now, as an adult, he could handle them
effectively and they were not going to destroy him. After working on this issue
for many months, he was freed up to be less fearful and he was able to reduce his
counting significantly.

From this example you can begin to see how and why feelings surface when
you are working to change things in your life, and also how positive and essential
they are when it comes to making these changes. In the remaining pages of this
chapter, I discuss some of the more common emotions that people experience
during this process.

LOSS, HURT, AND GRIEF

Feelings of loss, hurt, and grief often arise when you begin to look at your past and present and try to come to terms with it. Feeling hurt often arises from experiencing a loss. It could be the loss of a person from death, distance, or other factors. It could be the loss of someone's attention or love (like parents, friends, or partners), the loss of a trust, or the loss of a sense of self. These feelings are painful and much energy is usually spent trying *not* to feel them. This, again, is a big factor in why we develop defense mechanisms, coping styles, and self-defeating behaviors. We don't want to feel emotional pain. Emotional pain is a lot scarier for most people to face than physical pain. Loss, hurt, and grief are possibly the most painful of all emotions to experience because they reach down to your very core. The pain can be tremendous and overwhelming at times. But it is important to keep in mind that if you allow these feelings to run their course, not trying to deny or distort them, they will lessen in intensity over time. Eventually, you will feel relief; the pain will not last forever. While you are in the midst of these feelings, remember how important it is that you allow yourself to feel them. But also remember that you will not always feel as bad as you do right at that moment.

Allow yourself to feel and try to gain understanding of where and when your feelings arose. Elicit the support of your friends, family, clergy, and therapist to help you through these feelings. Ask them to lend an ear so that you can talk about the pain and where it comes from. In addition to having others to help support you through this, it is a good idea to get a journal and write down your thoughts, feelings, and experiences. Sometimes we learn the most about ourselves just from writing in our journals. Let your journal be an important friend and confidant. The only way out of these feelings for good is not to go around them, but to go through them.

FEAR AND ANXIETY

Anxiety is the fear of a future event. It can be a real or an imagined event, both being very powerful. Anxiety could be a fear of a loss, the fear of something new, the fear of the unknown, the fear of a hurt, fear of embarrassment or humiliation, the fear of a change, or the fear of anything that makes you feel insecure. It can manifest itself in many ways, from mild apprehension and tension to panic attacks, involving dizziness, sweating, shaking, a fuzzy-headed sensation, blurred vision, heart palpitations, feeling unsafe, and feeling as if you are going crazy or are about to die.

I asked a patient of mine, Lori, to describe what her anxiety feels like to her. She said that she first gets a sense of feeling uneasy, agitated, and tense. Sometimes, she feels that something bad will happen out of nowhere and sometimes it is attached to an event (i.e. fearing that she will be lost in terrible disaster, such as a fire, a hurricane, or an earthquake). She has an irrational feeling that things are out of her control and are actively working against her. This creates intense anxiety for Lori.

When people think about and even begin to make changes in their lives, anxiety is present. Of course, they can be anxious—they are apprehensive about making these changes. It brings up lots of questions such as, "What is my life going to be like if I make this change?" "Can I really do it or am I setting myself up for another failure?" "What feelings will I have to confront if I make these changes and look into those hidden areas of my life?" Who wouldn't feel anxiety at the precipice of dramatic change? Sometimes, what you perceive as anxiety is actually excitement. Much depends on how you interpret your emotions. Obviously, it is more positive and easier to move forward if you interpret your feelings as excitement, rather than anxiety when you are about to make changes.

Anxiety can also be a mask for other feelings that are underneath it. If you are preoccupied with the anxiety, you don't have to feel what is underneath. It is important to face both the anxiety and the underlying feelings when you are in this process. The anxiety is usually the first feeling to arise. Underneath the anxiety is where pain, hurt, loss, grief, guilt, and anger reside. Anxiety is an uncomfortable feeling; there is no doubt about it. But do not let it scare you away from making the changes that you know are necessary in order for you to have a fuller, healthier, and more satisfying life. The more you push through your anxiety and confront your feelings directly, the less anxious you will be. Perceive anxiety as a signal that you are apprehensive about something. Explore what it is.

GUILT

Many people feel guilty when they begin a process of change. They feel as if they are somehow bad and do not deserve a better life. Or they feel that they will surpass the significant people in their lives and want to leave them, but feel too guilty doing so. They fear abandoning their partners because this would create tremendous feelings of guilt. They do not feel worthy or entitled to a better life. Their self-esteem is often tenuous and they tend to blame themselves and take responsibility for everything and everyone around them. They are often self-deprecating and may sabotage their efforts to change early in the process. People who tend to feel guilty will have a harder time with changing their negative self-concept because they really believe that they are bad and unworthy.

If you feel guilt, do not give into the negative messages that accompany it. Try to understand why you are feeling guilty and from where it originates. Unless you have committed a terrible crime against humanity for which remorse is appropriate, chances are, your feelings of guilt are undeserved. You probably suffer more from lacking the ability to acknowledge and express your anger. Believe it or not, this leads to feelings of guilt. Many people who have frequent feelings of guilt may find that they do not allow themselves to get angry with others. They may even have trouble admitting that they feel angry. They'd sooner punish themselves for all of their imagined ills than admit and express their anger to the people with which they feel a conflict. It is extremely difficult for people who feel guilty to directly confront a person toward which they have a long-standing anger. Since the feelings of guilt do not allow for the appropriate expression of anger, "guilt ridden" individuals may act out in a passive-aggressive manner in order to indirectly express anger.

Sue feels guilty all the time. She blames herself for not being a good enough mother, wife, daughter, and friend. She feels that her performance at work is not up to par, for which she also feels guilt. She feels that her husband places unrealistic demands on her to do all of the housework, childcare, and work full-time. Instead of expressing her feelings of anger toward her husband and telling him how his expectations make her feel, she acts in ways that do release some of the anger, but are not direct and often cause more harm than good. Sue is late whenever she and her husband need to go somewhere together. She sometimes does not make his dinner or do the laundry with the excuse that she lost track of time, or she will ignore him when he is calling her from another room and pretend she doesn't hear him.

She does this mostly unconsciously, but it is her way of expressing her anger. So while Sue is berating herself for being such a terrible person, feeling guilty about everything, she is seething underneath, but has not been able to express it. Why? Because she feels too guilty expressing it. She believes that if she feels angry and expresses it to her husband, she is an ungrateful and evil person, which just confirms her negative beliefs about herself. She thinks, "How can I be so selfish? He works hard too. I should just do a better job!" Do you see how guilt is a vicious cycle? Nothing constructive comes from it.

If you do something that is deserving of remorse, apologize to the person whom you hurt, express your remorse, and move on. Now that you understand a bit more about guilt, do not let yourself fall into the "guilt trap." That is exactly what it is, a trap. You can get caught in it and not be able to make the necessary changes you want to make. Work hard on combating the negative messages. It's all part of your personal peace process.

ANGER

Many of my patients who have gone through the process of change, subsequently looking into their past, report experiencing anger. They may not call it anger, but rather "being frustrated," "peeved," "annoyed," "bothered," or "ticked off." People who are angry and have difficulty acknowledging and expressing it often have a physical reaction—headaches, stomachaches, backaches, and nausea are some of the symptoms—but it is anger nonetheless. It is important to acknowledge and understand your anger.

> Andrea was furious with her best friend Kaye. Kaye was supposed to come to Andrea's graduation party, but at the last minute was unable to attend due to family constraints. Andrea was very angry with Kaye for missing her party, even accusing her of missing it on purpose. But underneath the anger, Andrea felt hurt and rejected. She felt hurt that Kaye didn't stand up to her family and tell them that she had previous plans. Andrea felt hurt because she felt that Kaye did not think that she was important or special enough. Her feelings were hurt, and instead of feeling the hurt, she felt intense anger.

For some, it is easier to feel anger than allow in the hurt feelings that leave us vulnerable. For others it is just the opposite. Some people find it much harder to allow their angry feelings, and would rather focus on the hurt. For them, the anger is too threatening. They may feel that expressing their anger may lead to abandonment by the object of their anger. So they bury their anger and focus on other feelings instead. Most of us were not taught how to constructively feel and deal with our anger. Thus, we were left with only maladaptive techniques.

In working toward your personal peace process, you may find yourself getting angry because you are remembering things about your childhood that are bringing up these feelings. Often, angry feelings that are smoldering inside stem from early childhood experiences. If you seem to be angry without any situational circumstances bringing it about, an examination of your relationship with your parents will often shine a light on the situation. Maybe you are remembering being the victim of abuse, or being unjustly accused of something, or simply not having things go your way. Your anger is a normal and a necessary response to those situations. It will help you make the changes you want if you use it in an effective manner, not a destructive one.

Anger can be used to educate yourself about your past or present situations. Just as we saw that anxiety can help you get to know yourself better and be used as a signal to alert you to the fact that you are on the road to change, anger can be utilized to enhance the quality of your life as well. As long as your anger is not directed at harming others or yourself, try to make sense of your emotions so you can understand and heal your wounds, and continue toward your personal peace process.

> Leo identified his anger with his wife as frustration. He did not want to be married to her and each day he avoided the dilemma, his anger mounted. It was not until he openly and honestly discussed the matter with his wife that his anger was abated. Discussing the issue in therapy, he concluded he owed her the chance to seek professional help before terminating the marriage. They sought couple's counseling and worked together on improving their communication and intimacy.

Sometimes, the degree of resentment some people feel is an indication of how much anger they are experiencing. Resentment usually exists when there are unresolved conflicts. Often, anger arises because a person feels abused or taken advantage of. It can also stem from jealousy and distrust. Those who have been badly hurt earlier in their lives tend to be angry more often than those who didn't experience such early trauma.

Keep in mind, anger is a normal emotion and need not be a problem if handled in an effective manner. The main issue is how and why we express or repress it. Many people find it difficult indeed to deal with anger in an effective and appropriate way.

> Jerry told me, "I get angry, but I never really do anything about it. Last weekend, I took my sons to the amusement park and some kids cut in line a few people ahead of us while we and all the others were waiting thirty minutes. I sure was angry, but I couldn't get myself to say anything to the kids for fear of making a scene, or looking stupid. Meanwhile, I'm sure my own boys were wondering why I didn't stop them."

Jerry was probably fearful of a confrontation. And clearly, he was angry with himself, too. He will keep those angry feelings inside and they will probably produce tension in the form of headaches, depression, or anxiety. If Jerry would only assert himself, his anger would disappear and he would have considerably more self-esteem. He would have felt proud of himself if he had calmly told the other kids that he and everybody else had been waiting in the line, and they had no right to cut in front. Anger held in will only smolder like burning coals.

People who are unable to assert their anger in an appropriate way, who hold back and repress it, can be prone to uncontrollable bursts of temper. Storing one's anger can cause feelings of inadequacy, tension, and depression. Most therapists encourage their patients to express their anger openly and honestly, rather than repress it. But ventilating your anger is not, by itself, the full answer to the problem. What's important is the manner in which you "let off steam." It can either pave the way to better understanding or it can result in further conflict. Whatever method is used, it should enable you to feel better about yourself. Again, find a family member, friend, or someone with whom you can share your feelings. If no one is available, write in your journal and vent. If you find that your anger is leading you to do destructive things to yourself or others, do seek professional help.

In this chapter, I have discussed some of the feelings that may arise as you begin and proceed through the very important work of making positive life changes. Some of these feelings can be painful and difficult. They will challenge you, but you are up for the challenge. You proved this by picking up and reading this far into the book.

Not all of the feelings that you will experience in your personal peace process are painful; some will be absolutely wonderful! As you make the changes you desire, you will undoubtedly also experience joy, relief, laughter, excitement, elation, satisfaction, contentment, and, finally, *peace*. The further you go through the process of attaining the life you seek, the more you will experience these positive feelings and the less you will experience the painful ones.

Chapter Eleven

MAKING CHANGE PERMANENT

WHAT IS SUCCESS?

In any major successful project undertaking, there is a sequence of steps or phases that needs to be performed. These basic phases include:

1.   Defining the problem or objective

2.   Establishing a plan

3.   Implementing the plan

4.   Maintaining and Improving

These phases are generic enough to apply to any kind of project, from building a skyscraper to learning to play the piano or a sport—they are the same for improving one's life, or embarking on a personal peace process. You've already defined the problem, established your peace plan, and put the plan into action. Once you've begun to make some of the short-and long-term changes you've identified in your goal worksheet, the maintenance phase needs to kick in.

In the case of building a skyscraper, the maintenance phase would include cleaning, upgrading carpeting and paint, replacing lighting when necessary, and upgrading electrical systems as appropriate. For learning piano, maintenance might be as simple as practicing and continuing to learn new techniques. For you, once you have begun to see positive changes, the most important thing will be to keep the progress and momentum going, and to be mindful of any potential relapses.

To learn to play football, one must be knowledgeable of every aspect of the game and do all that is possible to execute the skills required for his position with intelligence and determination.

PREVENTING RELAPSE

Individuals react differently as they begin to experience positive change in their lives. Some people feel guilty for feeling so good about themselves. Conversely, they may gain so much confidence in their ability to change that they think they don't need to work on changing anymore. The key to preventing relapse is to maintain awareness of your potential pitfalls. In previous chapters, we discussed the obstacles that could obstruct getting started on your personal peace process, and you learned various means of overcoming these blocks. Preventing relapse and maintaining change requires you to practice these same techniques over and over again. For instance, if one of the things you've changed is the way you deal with shyness, and you know that certain situations cause you to feel vulnerable, anticipate that the same coping styles or defense mechanisms may resurface, and plan ahead as to how you will deal with them more effectively than in the past.

> Stephen developed a plan for coping with his shyness at parties. He knew from experience that when he went to a party, he usually stayed close to whoever had accompanied him rather than mingling with others. He also tended to leave early. Through our work together he became aware of these tendencies and made successful efforts to change them. He no longer dreaded parties. However, he was also aware of his potential to revert back to his old shy behavior. Therefore, he developed a foolproof plan. He made himself speak to at least five new people before leaving a party, no matter how uncomfortable he felt. He even went so far as to come up with potential conversation-starters that he could use to break the ice with people he didn't know. By sticking to this plan, he avoided falling back into his erroneous ways of thinking about himself, which included thinking he was a social misfit. On the contrary, speaking to new acquaintances helped to enhance his self-confidence while at the same time opening him up to new relationships.

What do you have to do to come up with your own maintenance plan? First, think about all the different areas of your life. Are there any particularly risky areas in terms of reverting back to your previous ways of thinking and behaving? For example, does your workplace offer a challenge? How about your home life? Are there particular times of the year or places you have to go that cause difficulty for you? For example, do the holidays bring on certain feelings for you that will make maintaining your change a challenge? Is there anything you can think of to make these places or times easier to handle? By anticipating and planning ahead, you will be much better prepared to deal with issues as they develop.

In this chapter, we will review some techniques for recognizing and dealing with relapses. We will also discuss ideas on how to maintain an emotionally positive, healthy lifestyle. This is a section of the book that you may want to refer back to several times as you reach different levels of progress in your personal peace process.

WHAT TO DO WHEN RELAPSE OCCURS

Keep in mind that your success at being the way you want to be will get stronger as you continue to grow and change. The more you practice your new ways of thinking or behaving, the more firmly permanent they will become. But let's say you do relapse. Perhaps you find yourself thinking old, familiar self-defeating thoughts. Maybe you catch yourself making negative statements about yourself. Or perhaps you notice that you are reverting back to old ways of behaving due to the situation at hand. What do you do?

There are some common reactions people have after they relapse. For example, they may feel that they have failed, that maintaining change is a hopeless cause, and that they therefore should give up. Often, the person blames such a "slip-up" on him or herself and may feel that he or she is unable to succeed. Therefore, it is important to keep in mind that slipping is not a sign of your weakness, but is instead a signal that your coping skills still need further honing. Use these "slip-ups" as opportunities to learn. For example, if you feel yourself making negative statements about yourself, think about why this is happening. Examine how you are feeling and try to identify what it is that is causing you to revert back to your old familiar tendencies. After you can identify what is bothering you, you will be able to proceed intelligently from a position of strength. Decide how you can deal positively with the situation. Your approach should be to cope the best, most effective way you know, based on the successful experiences you have already had reaching your initial goals. You will come to view these relapse situations as rewarding challenges and opportunities to address your issues and become even stronger.

MAKING PERMANENT LIFESTYLE CHANGES

For some people, maintaining change requires establishing new lifestyle changes altogether. We all know that it is important to take care of yourself both emotionally and physically. From my observations, I have developed some general guidelines that I have shared with my patients to help them make their own changes permanent and long-lasting. Here are some ideas to consider:

1.   **Relationship Selection:** Pick your relationships carefully and re-evaluate them often. Only maintain those relationships that make you feel good about yourself. The people with whom you associate should give you something of value in return. It can be trust, laughter, or simply some effective communication; but it should be something beautiful, relevant, and meaningful to both parties. If you find yourself in relationships where you are taken advantage of, or are discriminated against, ridiculed, or treated unfairly in any way, get out of that relationship. The people and activities that you associate with should enhance your self-respect, not destroy it. If you befriend someone who is primarily concerned with his or her own needs at your expense, you will feel cheated. You will not grow, and you will only end up being angry with yourself and feeling frustrated. These feelings will make it difficult to maintain the positive changes you have made for yourself.

2.   **Activity Selection:** The same concept applies to your other free-time activities. Be selective about what you do with your time. Pick the books you read carefully, and use good judgment. If you are wasting your time watching meaningless TV or reading books that do nothing but use up your time, make a change for something better. Look for those books that will expand your mind, expose you to new areas of learning, or help you to think differently. If you are involved in extracurricular activities that do not give you pleasure, drop them. If you feel you are over-extended in your social commitments, prioritize them and decide which ones to maintain and which to get rid of. In general, be discriminating in all areas of your life. Do not stay with an activity simply because you feel you must. Your time is too valuable to be wasted. Lost time is never found.

Remember, each time you do something new, you become someone new. Your life is enriched and expanded; you become a more interesting person to yourself and to others. Do not be afraid of experimenting.

3.   **Practice Creativity:** Do something creative. Every person has talents—even you. If you are saying to yourself that you have none, it is simply that yours have not been discovered. If you let your imagination wander, you can come up with an unlimited supply of activities that can be most challenging and rewarding.

Have you thought about taking a course, learning an instrument, or joining a reading discussion group? What about learning to paint or draw, or joining a group such as hiking, skiing, theater, speaking, singing, or any type? Whatever you choose, the idea is to find something that you enjoy and that gives you a sense of accomplishment. If a new activity makes you feel good, it reduces the possibility of falling into those old familiar ways of being.

4.   **Maintaining Assertiveness:** In previous chapters, I've spoken about the importance of becoming more assertive and standing up for yourself. It is not only important for the protection of your rights and needs as an individual, but aids in maintaining the changes you have established. Practice your assertiveness whenever possible, keeping in mind the fine line between being assertive and being aggressive.

5.   **Exercise:** We all have several types of energy—one is the energy required to concentrate on a book, another is the energy required to walk, play tennis, or swim. The person who physically exercises regularly will require less effort to do something physical. Additionally, that person will be in better shape to withstand any physical stress on the body as well as any emotional stress on the mind. By reducing stress, you will be better able to maintain the changes you have incorporated into your life. My patients who physically exercise on a regular basis are less vulnerable to becoming upset. Also, they seem to cope with stress better than the patients who do not exercise. Any physician will tell you exercise has a multitude of physiological benefits. Make regular physical exercise a part of your routine, a part of your life. Pick up an exercise book, video, or seek the advice of a trainer if you do not know what to do. If the "old you" complained of not having the time, being bored, being too tired from work, or too old to exercise, overrule the "old you" and say, "I'm going to exercise regularly because it's good for me and I need to stay healthy." Part of my regular routine is going to the gym five days a week.

You know yourself better than anyone does, and you know the things that will best be able to help you maintain the changes you have already made while at the same time allowing you to continue to achieve your long term goals. It's important to see yourself as a winner, especially during this period of making your changes permanent. A positive attitude is critical if you are to realize lifelong successes. Put yourself into situations that offer opportunities for acquiring greater confidence and skill.

PART FOUR

YOUR EMOTIONS AND FEELINGS

Chapter Twelve

DEALING WITH DEPRESSION AND ANXIETY

Because a high proportion of the patients I have seen over the years came to me with problems related to depression and/or anxiety, I have devoted the first chapter of this section to these two topics. Most of the ideas I will share center on analyzing how you think, and then exploring new ways of thinking that will replace thoughts that are damaging. These ideas and techniques have worked successfully for many of my patients. They may or may not apply to you specifically, but even if they don't, they may generate ideas for you that are more applicable to your own situation. There should be no shame or embarrassment associated with feeling depressed. In fact there are a multitude of cases of depression that have a biologic etiology and are treatable with medication and psychotherapy. A careful diagnosis of the root of the depression is imperative.

When I ask troubled patients how they are feeling, they often don't know what to say, possibly because they are feeling several emotions at once. They may feel inadequate, hopeless, frightened, or even guilty. The problems of depressed people are usually centered on their thoughts and feelings rather than their actions. They are often feeling pessimistic and thinking self-deprecating thoughts. They readily find fault with themselves. If you can relate to these descriptions, ask yourself the following questions: How often do I feel down? How long does the mood last? How much does it interfere with my life? Do I ever feel like giving up?

There is such a thing as reactive depression, especially when something tragic occurs in your life. When my father died suddenly of a cerebral hemorrhage, I went into shock. Many months after his death, I still felt great sadness. While it did not interfere with my work or family life, I felt the loss deeply. I have also seen patients whose children were killed accidentally, whose homes were destroyed by fire, who lost their jobs, whose mates left them, or who lost all their money. All these people had good reasons for feeling depressed. Life was indeed treating them unfairly, and they were reacting normally. If you have experienced such a trauma recently, or are going through a period of severe loss, you should expect to feel a major change in mood (i.e. depression).

There is, however, a more lasting type of depression in which symptoms may range in severity from feeling mildly disturbed to being suicidal. These symptoms include feelings of loneliness, boredom and apathy, crying too much, sleep disturbance, helplessness, hopelessness, and more. Suicide, obviously, is the result of extreme depression. Unfortunately though, suicide is a permanent solution to an often temporary problem. Not to belittle the problems people have that lead to depression, but I have always identified with a proverb borrowed from the French: *Après le plui, il fait le bon temps.* Or, after the rain, comes the good weather. Often, when time passes, what seemed a monumental blow at its onset, is not as debilitating after we've had a chance to regroup, repair the damage, and move on.

What can the average person do to fight depression? First of all, if the symptoms are so severe that they are affecting one's ability to function, or if there are suicidal thoughts involved, see a psychologist, psychiatrist, or social worker immediately. For those with less severe symptoms, it is helpful to learn how to control the symptoms.

What we have learned from research and the treatment of millions of patients suffering from depression is that people can and do change. Many emotional problems are learned; that is, they are the result of unmet emotional needs stemming from childhood. The good news is, what has been learned can be unlearned. One of the most successful treatments is to teach people to control their thoughts. This may sound overly simplistic, but it's true. We have demonstrated time and time again that depression decreases when patients are induced to think more positively about themselves. The next time you're feeling depressed, examine your thoughts. Chances are, you are thinking negatively. Most likely you are drawing inaccurate perceptions about yourself.

> Alan was not doing well in school. He claimed that being depressed caused him to be unable to study or interact in class. When I asked him what he usually thought about, he could say nothing positive about himself. He felt, for example, that if he participated in a classroom discussion he would be wrong and the subject of ridicule, so why try?

If you are facing similar problems, stop concentrating on what you think is wrong with you. Instead, try thinking about what's good, and even great, about yourself. Make a list of your good attributes. Remind yourself of those things that you like about yourself. You may have been told you're witty or engaging, or perhaps you've always liked the shape of your nose. It doesn't matter what you come up with, but write these thoughts down. If you can't come up with any, ask someone close to you that you trust to tell you what they like about you.

It is important to keep these good qualities in mind, so that any time you think poorly of yourself, you can replace that thought with a good one about yourself. Each time you say something to yourself that is negative, limiting, or damaging, replace the thought with a positive one. The idea is to disprove or discredit the part of you that is sending the negative message.

Here are some examples:

NEGATIVE SELF-TALK	POSITIVE SELF-TALK.
I am not as attractive as most men/women.	I have been told I have beautiful eyes.
I am not a good dancer.	I can take lessons and improve. Also, I am an accomplished writer.
I am not smart enough.	When I've put my mind to things in the past, I have done very well.

Keep in mind that the key to reversing negative statements is to let your dominant positive thoughts prove there is little truth in the negative assumptions. Practicing positive self-talk will condition you to use new ways of viewing yourself as well as perceiving stressful situations. The more you practice positive self-talk, the sooner you will feel differently about yourself. Eventually, you will feel more relaxed and more confident.

You might think the solution to reducing depressive feelings sounds simple. Believe me, the method is effective. Work on substituting positive thoughts about yourself in place of your old, entrenched negative perceptions. Begin by viewing the depression you're feeling as a warning signal. Examine the times you get depressed and try to determine what preceded the depression. Instead of continuing to feel down, think in terms of using it as a signal to better your life, not a time for feeling helpless and hopeless.

One antidote for depression is to keep busy. People who feel depressed tend to become preoccupied with their problems. They create too much free time for themselves. Be sure to include a lot of interesting things to do each day. Exercise, maintain social relationships, and don't focus too much attention on yourself. At the same time, be realistic about the activities you choose. Don't make demands on yourself that can only worsen what you are trying to fix. Another good way to avoid or reduce depression is to do something for others. Taking an interest in and helping another person can do a great deal for your ego.

Frequently, when I ask people what they look forward to in life, I get in return a half-smile and a vague response. Upon exploring the topic more deeply, I learn that they would like to do a lot of things—take a course, travel, change jobs, and so on. When I ask what is holding them back, they say they are waiting for the "right time" or enough money. Action is the keyword here. Find a way to do what you want to do without all the excuses. You'll be amazed how this will chase away your negative feelings.

REDUCING ANXIETY

Some of the most common problems faced by my patients are related to anxiety. By anxiety, I am not talking only about panic attacks and specific phobias, but also about the more general consequence of anxiety, which is the tendency for many people to avoid situations because they provoke uncomfortable feelings. There are many factors relating to the cause of anxiety, including a heredity-based predisposition toward anxiety, and the influence of developmental experiences. Early parental programming can bring about insecurities that result in an individual's increased fragility. I believe that heredity deals the cards and environment plays them. Although we cannot rule out biological factors, conditions, such as anxiety, often are repeated from generation to generation because children learn from their parents.

Having analyzed the parental influences of my patients with anxiety, I have found that many could not depend on their parents for emotional support, or else were raised to feel overly dependent on their parents. Either way, their developmental experiences contributed to present feelings of anxiety that affected their ability to experience happiness or peace to the fullest extent. The following examples demonstrate how parental influences may manifest themselves as anxiety symptoms.

> Bruce, thirty-one years old, experienced considerable anxiety regarding his inability to complete his doctorate in history, although his job demanded that he attain a doctoral degree. His fear of public speaking made him feel he would never be able to defend his dissertation.

"I am a lot like my mother, who is a worrier and a fearful lady. When I was a child, she told me so many things to be on the alert for, I was scared as hell. You feed all that garbage to a kid and it messes up his mind. She constantly told me things like 'Thunder and lightning will kill you,' 'Keep the shades down, because if robbers see what we have they will steal from us.' One time, I rode my bike to a friend's house two blocks from where we lived and she took the bike away forever. My mother said she didn't want me getting hit by a car. She made me crazy. I was starting to see danger everywhere."

Bruce had all of his academic work completed for a doctorate except his dissertation. In therapy, he talked about his overwhelming fear of failing his oral examination since it required public speaking. When an individual grows up receiving the message that danger is around every corner, it is very easy to develop overwhelming fears, or phobias. Any natural courage that we are all born with is dissipated when a person is taught to fear the unknown. Bruce had taken on his mother's anxiety to the point where it interfered with his professional goals.

Jan came for help because she was anxious and experiencing difficulty breathing. She reported that she could not relax and felt tightness in her chest. "I can hear my heart beating," she explained. Jan was forty-five, married, and the mother of two sons. She had experienced difficulty maintaining various waitressing jobs because she repeatedly made careless mistakes. She complained that she often felt too overwhelmed to perform her job carefully. As a result, she was often fired soon after starting a job.

"I was thinking about why I'm a nervous wreck. I'm too old to be blaming my parents for my problems, but they did a lousy job as parents. They're not drunks, but the evenings were ruined by the usual daily gin and tonics. You couldn't talk sense to my parents at night. If you wanted help with homework, forget about it. If you had a problem, you kept it to yourself."

It didn't sound as if Jan could depend upon her parents for guidance, love, or understanding. As a result, she rarely felt completely "safe" because she didn't perceive her parents as providing security. Her lack of interaction with them unquestionably contributed to her being a frightened, anxious person.

Tom, a physician, told me he was very tense. He'd sought help because he was fearful that he would make a mistake in his work and somehow harm a patient.

I should have come for help years ago. I'm more than a tense person. I know anxiety when I see it. Don't let the doctor title fool you. I've got all the signs, from my fears to a very rapid heartbeat. I just don't know how to change it."

Asked to talk more about the origin of his anxiety, Tom reported the following:

"I don't think my parents should have had children. They can't handle their life. They were not happy together and they are not happy as individuals. As a child I felt like I didn't have parents. We interacted mechanically. Even when I was with them, they were doing their own thing. I felt rejected when I was with my mother. She was always reading and too busy for me. My father wouldn't miss a golf game under any circumstances. He was never interested in what I was doing and never had time for me."

In therapy, Tom was able to see that he had always tried to gain his parents' attention by focusing on his academic abilities. He attended medical school because he thought it would make his parents proud of him, yet he was never able to develop pride in himself. It didn't matter how accomplished he became since he still felt unloved by his parents.

As you can see from these examples, symptoms of anxiety are usually due to inaccurate thoughts that become conditioned. Bruce, for example, had convinced himself not to proceed with his professional goals because doing so entailed the risk of failure. Jan became conditioned to keep her thoughts to herself or risk feeling angry. Tom lacked confidence in himself and his abilities. Each of these people was suffering from the effects of anxiety because they believed the negative messages they received as children. They were all repeating these negative messages to themselves over and over as adults, even though the messages were unrealistic. As a result, they were being held back from experiencing the lives they wanted to lead.

The good news is, all of these patients that I have described to you were eventually able to overcome the effects of anxiety that were interfering with their happiness. For some, the change was relatively quick and easy; for others, change came a bit more slowly. Nevertheless, I can tell you that they all feel more satisfied with themselves. So how were they able to do it?

One particularly effective method of reducing anxiety is *stress inoculation training*. This is a cognitive behavioral tool that involves both skills training and modification of maladaptive ways of thinking. Stress inoculation training is quite easy, and you can practice it on your own. First, you have to think about all the ways in which you perpetuate your own inaccurate thoughts. To do this, you must analyze your self-talk. As psychologist Albert Ellis, Ph.D. once observed, we all engage in self-talk. We all talk to ourselves, in that thoughts are always running through our heads. Some of these thoughts are maladaptive and they do not help us to be the person we want to be. However, if you can learn how to monitor your unique thought patterns, you can control your behavior as well.

In simple terms, our negative thoughts are what cause us to feel bad. However, these thoughts are usually unrealistic. Thinking leads to behavior. If, for example, you find that you frequently engage in self-deprecating thoughts, you may also be engaging in self-destructive behaviors stemming from those thoughts. By understanding how you think, you can begin to change how you behave. This process does take time, so for now, simply concentrate on becoming an observer of your own self-talk. As you start to reflect on how you think, consider the case of Ned, forty, who entered therapy because of anxiety and depression.

An employee in a small manufacturing firm, Ned had recently been abandoned by his wife. Although the failed relationship had shaken him, his problems appeared to be deeply rooted. In his self-talk, he was waging war with himself. Troubling thoughts constantly intruded. Asked what thoughts he was having lately, he explained: "What don't I think about? My thoughts are always racing, telling me that there is something wrong with me—that I look funny, or that I have said the wrong thing. I'm always worried. I keep thinking that my boss will fire me, even though I somehow manage to perform well on the job. How do I get all these negative thoughts out of my head? You must think I'm crazy."

By now, you are aware of the fact that your thoughts affect how you feel. You cannot continue to send negative messages to yourself and expect to reduce anxiety. You need new messages. Note the difference between the following healthy and unhealthy messages and try to think of new, positive messages you can substitute for the old, negative ones.

Old Message	New Message.
"What will people think if I get nervous?"	"I'm not concerned with what people think. I need to face my fears."
"I think I am going to have a breakdown."	"Being scared doesn't mean I am losing control."

"I've got to get out of here before
something happens."

"I have to stick this out and
become stronger."

Remember that we all have an automatic way of responding. We need to think about which automatic responses require modification. Keep in mind that you want to feel better. Your thoughts control your feelings. More specifically, how you perceive a given situation is the key. Imagine you are kept waiting on the phone to get directions to a friend's house. You can think unhealthy thoughts and get upset or you can think positively and feel relaxed. Which of the following examples is your usual reaction to such a situation?

A) "He's got a hell of a nerve keeping me waiting so long. My time is just as important as his is. I don't even feel like going."

B) "He will save me a lot of time by checking the map. He's apparently not familiar with the best roads for me to take. It's nice that he wants to see me."

This example is meant to demonstrate a specific idea: many times, our reactions to situations are all a matter of how we interpret them.

As another example, read what Kevin says about himself:

"I know I treat myself badly. It happens so fast and often it has become a part of me. I automatically put myself down. I not only do that, but always anticipate the worst. For instance, recently, a big super highway was built near where I live that could save me a lot of time going to work. Do I use it? No! Because I tell myself I'll get lost and be late for work. So I take the old road to be sure. It makes me mad that I'm so stupid."

That type of self-talk will keep Kevin anxious. He also worries about many other things that keep him on edge. He worries about being sick and dying, about people not liking him, about having a car accident and other dangers.

Another factor that contributes to anxiety is for a person to draw fallacious negative assumptions, especially about themselves.

David, for example, was promised a raise by his boss, and when several scheduled meetings with the boss were canceled, David assumed he would be fired. He convinced himself that his boss was seeking a replacement for him. Eventually, the meeting took place, during which his raise was discussed, as well as a pension plan. Needless to say, David was quite surprised. Speaking about the matter, he commented, "I really thought my boss didn't like me and considered me incompetent."

Negative parental tapes are not the sole reason mistaken beliefs exist. Individuals also learn them from peers, teachers, relatives, and from life's experiences. They are accepted as if they are fact, but they often are not. Many times, negative self-perceptions stem from feelings of insecurity and a lack of confidence. My guidance counselor in high school repeatedly told me to quit school and go to work. "School is not for you," he told me. Fortunately for me, I was able to prove him wrong.

Not too long ago I participated in the inauguration of the new president of Columbia University. There was a group of people assisting the assembly of colleagues, presidents, and dignitaries in putting on their academic robes. As a young lady straightened my hood, she asked, "Are you someone important?" I immediately replied, "Yes, I am," and then I added, "And you are somebody important too." The primary point here is that each person has importance and dignity just by virtue of the fact they exist. Life's accomplishments are a bonus added to our many individual qualities and strengths. It is important for each one of us to keep in mind all of our personal strengths. Similarly, it is important to try and rid yourself of the negative tapes that we all play in our heads.

SELF-CONTROL TECHNIQUES

Lastly, many of my patients have responded favorably to techniques such as *self-monitoring, thought stopping,* and *guided imagery.* They are described as follows:

Self-Monitoring

With this technique, an individual is instructed to record and chart a certain unwanted behavior every time it occurs. Doing this provides a record of the frequency, duration, and antecedents of the particular behavior. For example, Patti came to me wanting to stop her compulsive cleaning habit. She complained that she was spending an inordinate amount of time cleaning and straightening up—so much that she was vacuuming her house anywhere from three to ten times a day.

In addition to exploring the possible causes of her behavior, I encouraged Patti to keep a record of every time she felt the urge to vacuum. Doing this made her stop before actually carrying out her desire to vacuum. It also provided a paper record of how much time her urges were taking from her day. By the end of six weeks of self-monitoring, she had significantly reduced her vacuuming to where it was no longer controlling her life.

Thought Stopping

This technique is often used for controlling obsessive thoughts and ruminations. Just as it sounds, with this technique an individual is encouraged to obsess about a particular idea until the therapist yells out "Stop!" at which point the patient is startled into stopping. After a number of practice sessions, the patient is instructed to practice thought stopping without the therapist's assistance, at first out loud and then silently.

John came to me very upset over a recent breakup with his girlfriend of four years. He found that he was obsessing about the relationship so much that it was affecting his functioning at work. He complained that he couldn't stop thinking about his ex-girlfriend, so I practiced thought stopping with him and instructed him to practice it on his own. Within two weeks, John reported that he was no longer obsessing, had been able to replace his ruminations with healthier thoughts, and felt more in control of his life.

Guided Imagery

Imagery techniques are often used by therapists to increase a patient's feelings of self-control. For example, a therapist might guide a smoker by instructing him to visualize a police officer standing next to a stop sign anytime he or she feels the urge to smoke. Similarly, a smoker might visualize himself as a non-smoker. For instance, he would imagine himself waking up smoke-free, enjoying his morning coffee without a cigarette, putting on clothes that do not smell of smoke, and taking deep breaths without coughing. Guided imagery is very similar to the visualization techniques described in chapter eight, "Putting Your Plan into Action."

Chapter Thirteen

COPING EFFECTIVELY WITH GUILT

Guilt is a complex emotion. It usually comes into play when we feel we've done something wrong. It doesn't mean that we necessarily did do something wrong, but we feel that we have. Like depression, there are times when guilt is justified and times when it is not.

When a person steals, does an injustice to others, cheats, or lies, guilt often follows.

Lucy came to see me because she felt down and ashamed of herself. She had been very happy about climbing the ladder of success at work and becoming one of her company's youngest vice presidents. She was being given the red carpet treatment, and for good reasons. Clients reacted favorably to Lucy's charm, wit, responsiveness, and her ability to handle difficult situations.

As one of her "perks" at the bank where she worked, Lucy was given a credit card for business purposes only. Thinking her position was secure and her expenditures would not be checked, she began charging personal things to her account. As the months went on, she took even greater liberties, until one day she was called into the president's office and told she was dismissed. She was advised to select another profession and be thankful that the bank was not going to press charges. Lucy felt shocked and terribly guilty. She had used such poor judgment and violated her own basic code of honesty.

Feeling guilty about this is a healthy response. It will hopefully be enough to teach Lucy that there are grave consequences for her actions.

GUILT IS A BI-PRODUCT OF A POOR SELF-CONCEPT

Another type of guilt is found frequently among those who do not feel good about themselves.

Ed had grown up with a father who was excessively moralistic. As a minister, Ed's father wanted his son to be a model child. After all, the preacher's son should set an example for the other children. To make matters worse, Ed's mother was very critical of him. As a result, Ed grew up with the impression that he never did anything right, and his sense of guilt over not being able to please his parents was intense and constant. It got to the point where he felt bad about his performance in all areas of his life. He even imagined he had done things for which he should feel guilty, and he anticipated rejection around every corner.

"I'm a mess," he asserted at our first therapy session. "I'm scared and guilty about everything. These feelings didn't just start recently though, they go way back. I remember going to religious school and my father told the teacher to make sure I behaved. I didn't dare move in class, I was so scared of what would happen. All my life I tried to please my parents, but I could never make the grade. If my sister and I each bought them a gift, hers was the one they got all excited about. If something got broken in the house, I always got blamed. If I brought home a decent report card, it was never good enough. When my sister got her driver's license, they bought her a car. I got a bike.

"Now that I'm on my own and working," he continued, "things are no better. I even feel guilty getting paid because I feel that I don't deserve it. I think I do a lousy job. If there's a problem at work, I either assume I caused it, or I am afraid I'll be blamed for it. I'm forever anxious, fearful, or humiliated about something. It's like someone inside of me is saying, 'You're no good. You're a loser.' I think, 'How could anyone like me?'"

Ed raises a good question. How could anyone like him when he perceived himself as so unworthy? How could he not feel guilty when his self-esteem was so very low? After examining Ed's background, it was not hard to understand why he felt so poorly about himself. The product of insecure parents, he had not been programmed to feel worthy. In fact, he had done nothing to feel guilty about, but being so weak emotionally, he learned to blame everything that went wrong on himself.

I had a female patient with a similar background who got into a minor automobile accident and was threatened with a lawsuit. Despite her attorney's repeated attempts to assure her it was a routine case and would be settled easily, she became obsessed with the thought that the worst was about to happen. She feared that the accident would be perceived as her fault, and she imagined that she was going to jail and would lose her license. She felt all this needless guilt because she was so insecure and so vulnerable. Like Ed, she was listening to that same negative parental tape playing in her mind's ear: "You caused the accident. Somehow it must have been your fault." Is it any wonder that she would blame herself automatically for every bad thing that happened?

I constantly tell parents not to make their children feel guilty because guilt is not easy to get rid of. And I tell all my patients there is no such thing as a "bad" person. Even people who engage in unacceptable behavior are not bad; it's their actions that may be bad. It is unhealthy for a person to think in terms of being a lesser person. It is not possible to achieve a life full of purpose, happiness, and personal peace if you are convinced you're a "bad" person.

The first step in abolishing unhealthy guilt is to differentiate between things that you should feel guilty about, and the guilt simply carried around because you are not a confident person. If you are feeling guilty over something that happened many years ago, chances are, it is excess baggage that should be dumped. You don't need it. I recently saw a woman who still felt guilty about a "C" she had been given fifty years ago while attending college. When I asked her why she still felt guilty about something that happened so long ago, she replied, "I should have studied harder. After all, my parents were paying for that course."

Another woman I know feels very guilty because she has doubts about every incident involving the people in her life. "Do you think I ought to call Alice and apologize for serving sandwiches?" she'll wonder. Or, "Do you think the gift I gave Everett was too inexpensive?" This woman needs to explore what lies beneath her guilt.

If you've really done something to feel guilty about, such as forgetting to invite a good friend to a party, call your friend and speak honestly to him or her. If you are carrying around some old guilt, start thinking about who in this world sent the message that you should feel that way. It doesn't make any difference if the message came from your husband, your mother, or your uncle. You decide if you really did something so terrible that you should go around punishing yourself. Chances are the answer will be "no."

TAKE IT EASIER ON YOURSELF

Another good maxim is, "Don't make your code of behavior so strict that it doesn't leave room to be flexible." We need to be able to think and act without rules so rigid that no room is left for errors, for forgiveness, for another chance to try again. Life is similar to a game of tennis where there are repeated opportunities to make amends for past failures and find success.

> After several years of being a stay-at-home mom, Celeste, with her husband's encouragement, finally went back to work. She was long overdue to seek a challenge outside the home. She enjoyed her new career very much, but she kept worrying about neglecting her family.

Celeste felt this way despite the fact that she was unquestionably a dedicated wife and mother. The only thing her worries were producing was unnecessary guilt. When she realized that working was a healthy outlet for her and that, because of it, she would become a more fulfilled person, her guilt diminished.

> In another example, when I first saw Margie, she was still, at thirty-five, emotionally tied to her mother. She was very angry that her mother was able to make her feel guilty and influence her so much. Margie complained, "I have a good deal of difficulty pleasing my mother. She always makes me feel like I'm a bad child. I can never do enough for her. She doesn't like the way I discipline my children, the way I talk to my husband, what I wear, the friends I associate with, or how I spend my money. Every time I visit her I get the feeling I'm the worst person in the world."
>
> After Margie had been in therapy a while we were talking about the Steinway piano that had been in the family for years. Margie's mother had been telling her for months, "Of course, you are going to put it in your living room. It would get ruined anyplace else."
>
> "You should have heard me talk to my mother," Margie reported. "You would have been proud of me." I asked if she were proud of herself. "Proud is not the word!" she exclaimed. "Ecstatic would be more like it. I think Mother is finally getting the message that she will not intimidate me. She can no longer tell me what to do. When the piano came, I put it in the den as I intended to do. Mother said that if she knew it was going in the den she would have kept it, because now it will get ruined. I told her I did not agree with her, and that I expected

her to acknowledge my maturity and intelligence. I also told her to think carefully before she gave me anything again, because if she is going to give me things with strings attached, she can keep them. She saw I was plenty angry. She is not used to that. I think she's beginning to understand that she can't keep putting me on those guilt trips any more. I told her I was a damn good person and daughter, and that she'd better learn to appreciate me. She looked at me hard and said, 'Oh, I do think you are a wonderful person. I tell that to all my friends.' I told her I never got that message and repeated some of the many criticisms she had laid on me over the years. I told her exactly how terrible she had made me feel. Finally, she said, 'I never realized I was doing that to you.' I guess the big thing that has happened," Margie concluded, "is that I finally feel in control and so much less guilty about everything. I won't buy into that way of thinking any more. I have no reason to feel so guilty. I realized it was a way that my mother used to keep control of me. But this will not happen any more. I know that my mother still has some problems with this, but we'll be all right now that I know how to take care of myself when these things arise. I have to assert myself with her in order to feel like an independent, grown-up person."

ACKNOWLEDGE, BUT MOVE ON

Another typical example of guilt is magnifying something in your past to the point where you still worry about it today. Another patient I saw continued to feel guilty because she had cheated on her husband twenty years before. He had been dead for ten years. I asked her to think about what possible purpose it could serve to feel such guilt after so many years. She began to see that her indiscretion had been, in reality, a mere speck on the fabric of a beautiful marriage. Certainly, it was not worth the mental anguish she was enduring. We all have things in our backgrounds that can produce guilt. The point is, you should concentrate on what is good about you now, not something bad that happened in the past.

To sum up my antidote for guilt: try to see yourself as a good person, and think and act in a self-respectful way. If you try hard to live the best life you can, you'll be less prone to feel guilt under any circumstances because there will be no reason for it.

You should feel guilt if you deliberately or carelessly do something to harm another person, but unjustified guilt is a heavy load to carry. When we feel guilt for hurting someone, our conscience lets us know about it. Guilt that exists merely because one feels insecure and inadequate is debilitating and can cause a lot of emotional unrest.

Be on the alert for guilt feelings from the past. People should not suffer forever for past deeds. If you have done something that produced guilt, forgive yourself and don't repeat that behavior. Do not continue to punish yourself.

> Lori tells an interesting story about feeling guilty: "I don't know another person who carries around guilt to the extent I do. The thing is, I know I'm hard on myself and I'm not the bad person my parents said I was. But when you are a little kid, all that critical stuff sticks to you like glue. As I think of it now, I was in a no-win situation. No matter what I did, it wasn't acceptable. What finally got to me was their comparing me to every kid they knew. They were constantly saying, 'Why can't you be like so and so?' Many times I felt like shouting, 'Why can't you be nice to me?'"

Children can readily be made to feel bad. They are very sensitive, and it is not easy to forget unhappiness stemming from childhood. But it can be done by recognizing you are not the same helpless, dependent person being subjected to that harsh treatment. To permit yourself to be badgered by the past is like paying for your car more than once.

Think of the role guilt plays in your personality. Do you permit it to hamper you by using it as an excuse for not being productive and at peace? Perhaps you expect too much from yourself and you have set standards that are unrealistic. Being perfect may be the ideal to try to achieve, but how realistic is it? Seek ways to praise yourself. It will do a lot for your peace process. Be on the alert for anyone (parent, wife, husband, boss) who attempts to make you feel guilty. Do not permit it to happen. Protect yourself and deal intelligently with the criticism of others.

Chapter Fourteen

UNDERSTANDING ANGER

Barry first came to see me with his wife because she threatened to leave him if he didn't get help. She said he was impossible to live with because he was angry all the time. She reported he fights with his friends, the people he works with, and often gets into conflict with sales clerks and waitresses. She said several times he has broken valuable things around the house and recently threw the television set because it was not working when he wanted to watch a game. Gwen, his wife, said it didn't take much to light his fuse. The least little disagreement or frustration could set him off. "I can't tell you how many times he has broken a door or kitchen cabinet."

Barry did not deny that he was often angry. He said he never stopped to figure out his personality, but thought he was a lot like his father. He said he assumed people were one way or another and he was the angry type. Because he believed his wife was serious about leaving him he agreed to come for help.

Barry had never given much thought to why he behaved the way he did. Asked if he viewed himself as different from other people he had this to say: "I don't know much about psychology. I don't even know if I'm so different from anybody else. If something isn't right I speak up and try to make it right. Gwen will be nice to a waitress even if she doesn't like the food. I tell them what I think. If it's not fit to eat, I say so. I think a lot of my anger is because I'm working for her father. He favors his son and we're supposed to be equal. I break my neck to please the old man and he always has complaints. His son can do no wrong. So I'm frustrated. I tried a few jobs, but they didn't work out. I always had trouble with people. Once I went into business with a guy who wasn't honest. That didn't last. Another time I had a partner who wanted to be my boss. He was supposed to be my good friend. Who can you trust?

"I'm forty-two years old and where am I? What do I have to show for working over the years? You want to know why I feel angry? Nothing seems to go right for me."

Obviously, there are a lot of issues bothering Barry and he hasn't begun to sort them out. It appears as if he is not the most confident, relaxed person, but rather one who has many unresolved difficulties that bring about argumentative, defensive behavior. His anger is not the usual variety most people encounter.

There is ample evidence that there are millions of men and women who are abused by angry mates, and there are untold numbers of children who are abused by angry parents. Family violence is indeed a major problem in our society.

Any physical or verbal behavior that is directed at hurting another is aggression. I believe it is learned. Research shows how children copy particular models and illustrates that we can learn aggressive behaviors by observing others. Certainly, there is sufficient aggressive behavior to be observed in family settings, in the media, and in society. Also children who have been rejected or abused in any way are often full of repressed and covert anger.

We know that individuals who harbor angry feelings usually need very little to bring about an automatic angry response triggered off by fear, frustration, or a perceived attack.

WHY WE EXAMINE ANGER

Anger is a predisposition to react in a specific manner to an upsetting situation. It can be a positive reaction, such as the anger one may feel when seeing an adult abusing a child. Or it can be negative, such as a woman striking her child in anger or a person responding inappropriately to being frustrated.

Chris suffered a heart attack because he covered up his angry feelings. Urged to get help, he would say, "I don't need to talk to anyone. When I get angry, I plan a vacation." Chris died young because he didn't realize that uncontrolled anger can be a killer.

Sarah turned her anger on herself. Not feeling much self-worth, she did self-destructive things, such as involve herself with men who abused her. Her misdirected anger caused her a life of extreme emotional distress.

Serge took his anger out on his family, always yelling at his wife and children. His wife finally left him. It took losing his family for him to realize he needed help.

Barbara says she's been angry her entire life. She reports that she has no friends and even her family stays away from her. She never sought help, despite saying, "My life is hell, but I'm too scared to see what's behind that anger. I've been protecting myself that way for so long, it's hard to change."

Anger is difficult to harness, but certainly worth the effort. It's the difference between being miserable and being happy. And even if you have used anger to your physical detriment or damaged your self-image in the past, you can still learn to deal effectively with your anger. As explained in previous chapters of this book, it is a matter of replacing unhealthy concepts with those that are constructive.

Just as anxiety can be used as a signal if harnessed in the right way, anger can be controlled and utilized similarly. Here are some examples of how anger can be dealt with in a positive manner:

Rodney consistently badgered his son to the point where his wife insisted he explore why he was so angry. Rodney discovered he was threatened by his son being an excellent student and thinker. He was actually fearful his son would think he was dumb and not respect him.

Fortunately for Rodney, he was able to make sense of his faulty thinking and work on his relationship with his son.

Don was often angry with his wife because she avoided sex. He went to bed angry each night, but he never confronted her. When I asked why they didn't speak about sex, he said he thought she wasn't strong enough to deal with the problem. This is what his wife Fran had to say: "Don was surprised when I agreed to come with him to see you, Doctor. He acts like I am not concerned about our lack of intimacy. I can tell you not having sex doesn't make me feel terrific as a woman. We have our own thoughts about the matter, but, for some reason, we don't share them with each other. I'm inclined to think the problem is his, and he's inclined to think it's mine. The truth is, we are both at fault. I can't deal with his anger. That silent treatment doesn't

make me feel like making love. But at least we both are clearly willing
to work at it."

Note how anger festers and grows when not attended to; yet, when anger is
dealt with constructively, people can move on and greatly improve their situation.

ANGER IN EVERYDAY SITUATIONS

Let's look at some typical situations that could make a person angry. Suppose
your boss is annoyed with you because he feels the report you gave him was too
hastily prepared. He expresses his disappointment and says that he has serious
reservations about your ability to handle the job. In such a situation, it would be
difficult for you to yell back. One doesn't readily yell at a supervisor. Let's assume
that the boss was correct, and you actually did turn in an inferior piece of work.
What if you said to the boss, "I am sorry you are disappointed with the report.
Actually, I did spend too little time on it. It was not my best effort. Perhaps I
didn't understand the importance of the report. In the future, I will clarify assignments and you may be assured of a superior performance."

I believe most bosses would react favorably to such a response and give you an
opportunity to redeem yourself without your feeling degraded. The lesson to be
learned here is that your goal is to treat yourself with respect no matter how the
other person treats you. You control your feelings of self-esteem. On the other
hand, by giving up control and becoming personally threatened, you are bound to
feel considerably worse and angry about the entire situation.

When John was referred for help, he was suffering from colitis,
a severe stomach disorder. Not being too sure of himself, he often
found fault with others. It was his way of having a reason not to social-
ize. He was full of prejudices and felt trapped in a neurotic marriage.
His feelings of guilt and inadequacy had imprisoned him. Rather than
resolving differences with people, he was prone to argue with them.
He also thought his code of ethics and behavior was superior to most
others.

What John had difficulty understanding was that his dissatisfaction with life
and all the injustices he felt subjected to were directly related to his weak perception of himself. Not being a happy person, he carried his baggage of self-dissat-
isfaction into situations, causing negative perceptions and poor interactions with

people. John's colitis was probably a direct result of his failure to deal effectively with his anger, which, in turn, stemmed from his feelings of worthlessness.

Patients often tell me they find it difficult to comprehend that a physical problem can be triggered by psychological factors. The truth of the matter is that many physical problems have a psychological basis. The emotions or stress one experiences can indeed have a significant effect on the physical as well as the psychological well-being of the person. You can probably identify some physical effects of strong emotions experienced in your daily life, such as the churning feeling in your stomach when you feel upset, or the warm, flushed feeling when you're embarrassed. All of us have felt the mild to severe headache that comes on after a long, tense day on the job or at home.

Recently, I attended a college basketball game at a large sports arena. Because it was in the middle of the week and it was a regular season game, I expected to sit relatively close to the court. The man at the ticket window assured me that my seats were good, but, in reality, they were far from the court. I was annoyed and felt I'd been treated unfairly. The arena was crowded by now and it took me a long time to make my way back to the same window where I'd bought the ticket. "These are terrible seats," I complained to the man. "They are nowhere near the court." He replied, "They're the best I have. The computer does not lie. Since I sold you those, I've been selling tickets three sections further back than yours." He suggested that I move closer after the game started. "Probably someone won't show up and you can use their seat," he advised.

Having decided that the computer and the ticket seller were objective, and that I was being treated fairly under the circumstances, I no longer felt annoyed. I knew that should I return later in the season for another game, I would order tickets in advance or get to the arena earlier. In other words, I would learn from my experience. And I had learned that my feelings of anger could be lessened if I found out the facts behind the situation.

RELATING ANGER TO CHILDHOOD EXPERIENCES

Recently, I observed this scene in the supermarket: A boy, about five years old, was standing in front of a display of toy trucks. He said, "Mother, I would like one of those trucks." She immediately said to him, "I told you I was in a hurry and not to ask for anything. You are a bad, greedy, spoiled boy and I am not going to buy you anything ever again." The look on the child's face was sad indeed. The mother was successful in sending several negative messages to the child. I imagine the child would be angry with his mother for speaking that way. However, he has to push his feelings inside and keep quiet. He knows that if he speaks up, he won't be loved.

Ted says he can trace his anger directly to his father. Here's the story: "I always knew my father wasn't pleased with me. I wasn't interested in sports as a participant or an observer, despite the fact that sports were a big part of my father's life. When we played together during my youth, it wasn't fun. He was always critical. He was forever teaching me something I didn't want to learn. He never took an interest in what I was doing. You would think he would be pleased that I was a reader and a good student.

"He would call me lazy because I wasn't enthusiastic about helping him around the house. The few times we worked together, we wound up fighting. I was never doing the right thing. He would say he was better off doing it himself. Yes, I'm angry because his negative attitude caused me a lot of pain. Now that I'm an adult, it's not fair to blame my father for whatever my problems are, but I always wonder if I would feel better about myself and him if he wasn't so critical."

Alice says her mother is the cause of her anger: "Nobody gets me angry the way she does. I think she made me a very dependent person by doing so much for me. She even did my thinking. She always told me she knew better. If I wanted the red dress and she wanted the blue, she would always cast a doubt in my mind as to why the blue would be better. She got me to the point where I was always wondering how she was going to react to what I did. It was like I was forever wondering if she would approve. It could be something small like purchasing an unimportant item in the store.

"As I got older, I became an emotional wreck. I wanted to be an adult, but I was often acting like a child. I was actually afraid to stand up to her. I never thought about it until I was asked in therapy what I was afraid would happen if I were to confront my mother. I guess I was afraid she wouldn't love me. Isn't that ridiculous?"

It is evident that anger can interfere with our ability to be happy. Some people can remain calm while handling potentially explosive situations. Others have *low frustration tolerance*. An example of this can be seen when a relatively minor irritant, such as being stuck in traffic or waiting in a long line at a restaurant, causes excessive anger. If you are a person who gets easily upset, who is often prone to anger, or who consistently finds fault with others, then this chapter can be especially important to you. If you have a short fuse and are ready to explode at the most minor irritant, your health (if not life) is definitely at risk.

ANGER IS A NORMAL EMOTION, BUT NOT ALWAYS HANDLED NORMALLY

To help understand the anger you may be feeling, think for a moment about whether you are a negative or positive person. Are you often opposed to what other people are thinking and doing? Angry people frequently do not fit in with the group. Some go to extremes in order not to participate or conform. Sometimes, the degree of resentment some people feel is an indication of how much anger they are experiencing. Resentment usually exists when there are unresolved conflicts. Often, anger arises because a person feels abused or taken advantage of. It can also stem from jealousy and distrust. Those who have been badly hurt earlier in their lives tend to be angry.

Whatever its cause, anger is a normal emotion and does not need to pose problems for people. The main issue is how we express or repress it. Many people find it difficult indeed to deal with anger in an effective and appropriate way. You may remember Stuart from chapter two. He had a real problem controlling his anger.

> Stuart once told me, "I pull no punches when I'm angry. I'm the boss in my factory and the employees know it. They say I'm hard-nosed and have a strong temper. It's true—I can yell and curse with the best of them. My employees are afraid of me, but they work or they get out."

Stuart had come to me because he suffered from high blood pressure, which his physician felt stemmed in part from an emotional conflict. He had not learned how to deal in a healthy way with his angers, and he was not aware of the destructive effects to himself and those around him.

> Marion, however, is the opposite extreme. She claims she never gets angry.
>
> "I accept people for what they are," she insists, "and I'm never disappointed." She says she goes through life without ever experiencing angry feelings because of that attitude. Marion was always told by her parents not to argue with them or with other adults. To feel loved,

she was forced to play the role of a "good girl." She was taught not to argue with people or complain. Above all, she was told, "It is not nice to raise your voice or get excited."

I remember an interesting experience I once had in Frank's barbershop. A man who had come in after me jumped into the chair just as it was my turn. That made me feel angry. He was not next, I was. Ordinarily, I would have politely said something to the man, but I held back. He had a troubled look on his face, and the barber gave me a serious look as if to say that he knew something and that I should be patient. After the man had left the shop, Frank said, "Thanks for being patient, Ken. That man just lost his mother."

Dealing with anger in our society can indeed be confusing. Finding the proper balance is the goal. We don't want to be too easy, lest people will take advantage of us. However, we don't want to be continually angry either. Making sense of our anger also has a lot to do with the situation. Angry feelings often stem from a feeling of injustice, whether real or imagined. The trouble is, suppose you blow up at your boss because you're convinced he is underpaying you. Your boss will probably turn defensive and angry. A better approach would be to tell him or her that you enjoy working there but feel that not having received a promotion in several years is causing you a problem.

Susan worked in a small office with Mabel, who was obviously favored by the boss. The two women often argued over Mabel's smoking habit, which Susan claimed was creating a health hazard for everyone else in the office. Susan was convinced that Mabel smoked intentionally to anger her. As a result, Susan would go home each night in an angry mood. Her complaints to the boss were fruitless, and so she finally resolved the problem the only way she could—by taking another job.

If you find yourself in a similar situation, where you feel you are being used or abused, get out of it. Remove yourself from the scene and find something better. Don't let anger and frustration rule your life. Do not let an unhealthy situation go on day after day, month after month, or for years.

It's important to separate what is making you angry from the person with whom you are interacting. I urge parents to love their children at all times, but to deal firmly with issues related to discipline without attacking their children's feelings of self-worth. For example, if you are reprimanding a child for not remembering to turn off the water in the bathtub, you should deal with that issue. Do not call the child stupid and irresponsible. I have also seen many couples cause a great deal of unrest in their relationships because they attacked each other's personalities need-lessly. You can avoid a lot of unnecessary and unpleasant scenes by discussing the issues in a calm and sensible way. Displays of anger and violence will only build stronger resentments.

EXTREME ANGER

There are people who carry around such strong or extreme anger, they are often in need of professional help. This explosive anger that is intended to hurt others or oneself is not considered normal anger. This behavior is almost always the result of negative childhood experiences.

Al was referred to me by the courts. He had been arrested for physically abusing his wife. This type of case where a person is ordered by the court to obtain help is not the psychologist's most cooperative patient. It often takes considerable time for the patient to talk about himself and understand the source of all that repressed hostility. And it is not unusual to find that a "wife beater" has a history of being subjected to beatings.

Al initially said he was sorry he hit his wife, but he didn't think it was necessary to have him arrested and kept away from the house. He admitted he has a history of abusing his wife and his promises to stop have not been kept.

Al said he was raised primarily by his mother, who worked full-time. His father and mother were divorced. He seldom saw his father, but remembers being hit by him. Often, he was left alone. His mother left the lights on and told him he shouldn't be afraid. He said he remembered calling his grandmother when he was frightened.

Asked if he considered himself an angry person, he said: "I have always been an angry person. The kids used to call me 'Mad Al' because I was always in a fight. Kids were afraid of me. They said I didn't fight normal—that I fought to hurt."

Al obviously was carrying around hostility that had been prevalent since his early years. That severe anger usually stems from parental abuse and rejection. During Al's early years, there were not any adults around to make him feel secure.

Another serious case illustrating how anger can get out of control is that of a twenty-seven-year-old man named Wallace, who drank to excess, took drugs, and intentionally burned himself with cigarettes. Although he gave the appearance of being calm and jovial, he harbored a great deal of resentment, especially toward his parents. Note what he had to say: "I always felt my parents didn't like me. They won't say that's true, but I was always a bother to them. What I did, what I said, *everything* about me bugged them. They never liked to be with me. To this day, I can tell I annoy them."

Wallace was brought to me by his sister, who had been urging him to get help for some time. She reported he could not keep a job, had no friends, and walked the streets most of the time. "What normal person burns himself with a cigarette?" she asked.

Wallace's behavior was peculiar in many ways. Unable to stand the hurt of parental rejection, he resorted to a rich fantasy life where he imagined happiness. However, he believed he was "crazy" because that is what he had been called. He also believed he was bad and lazy, and had proof of a life of failure. Asked why he burned himself, he said, "If you're bad, you should be punished."

LETTING ANGER WORK FOR YOU, NOT AGAINST YOU

Modern psychology teaches us that anger is either internalized or projected onto others. People who are unable to assert their angry feelings in a normal way, who hold back and repress their anger, are prone to uncontrollable bursts of temper. Storing one's anger can cause feelings of inadequacy, tension, and depression. We know that it is healthy to express anger openly and honestly, rather than repress it. But ventilating your anger is not, by itself, the full answer to the problem. What's important is the manner in which you "let off steam." It can either pave the way to better understanding or it can result in further conflict. Whatever method is used, it should enable you to take control of your reaction.

Sometimes, it serves no healthy purpose to get angry. Whatever has occurred does not have to annoy you if it is understood and you feel in control. You can practice a type of control that can make life a lot less stressful. The general idea is that no matter what the other person says or does, *you can control your reaction to it. You* are in charge. Another person cannot make you angry if you refuse to allow it. For example, let's say that I'm sitting in my office waiting for Mr. Smith, who called for an appointment earlier that day saying it was an "emergency" and he had to see me immediately. Since I already had a full schedule, I decided to stay late to see Mr. Smith, which meant I had to cancel an outing to see a play. When Mr. Smith failed to keep his appointment, I was not happy about it but did not become angry because that would not make me feel good. After all, it was my decision to agree to meet with Mr. Smith. I will have to deal with his absence when I speak to him again. I probably will never upset my schedule again to see him, so this situation is not likely to recur. The reasoning for this is that the unrest I would have created for myself (if I had become angry) would serve no worthwhile purpose; it would only complicate matters further.

Don't confuse this reaction with "turning the other cheek" or "looking the other way." Rather, I'm proposing new ways of reacting to anger-producing situations that will result in your feeling better, and your achieving personal peace.

Here is another example of how to control your anger:

> Lottie was angry with her husband, Tom, because he didn't want to go to a neighborhood party. She felt that their neighbors didn't give parties often and that it would be an insult not to attend. She told her husband that he was rude and insensitive, that he always had to have his way. Tom thought Lottie was blowing the situation way out of proportion. Besides, he would have preferred to watch their son play ball that day and he refused to accept his wife's negative interpretations. Upon thinking it over, Lottie decided that she didn't really mean to say all those negative things she said about Tom. She concluded that going to the party without Tom would make her feel out of place and insecure, and *that* was the true underlying cause of her anger toward him. "I'm a grown, independent woman," she said to herself, "and my stability and security do not depend on my being with my husband every single minute." And so she went to the party alone and he went to his son's game.

How many times have you seen a husband or wife in a conflict like that, each one positive that the other is the cause? Even trivial episodes can trigger major explosions when such times of mutual resentment prevail. Each partner is sure he (or she) is correct, so they both continue to operate under that assumption. The trouble is, in the process, they are destroying their relationship. I have always counseled people to turn anger into constructive acts.

> A middle-aged patient named Harriet, whose sister was an invalid in a nursing home, came to see me because she was angry.

Whenever Harriet failed to make her daily visit to the nursing home, her sister complained and carried on. For Harriet, who had young children and a home to care for, the situation became quite serious. Because Harriet lacked self-assurance, her sister had no trouble making Harriet feel guilty.

I tried to convince Harriet that she should divert the anger and guilt she felt into a more positive, constructive direction. When Harriet admitted that she didn't know how to cope with her demanding sister, I recommended that she "act out" a scene in which she appeared angry with her sister. She was to tell her sister that she was making unrealistic demands on her, that visiting the home every day meant she could not take proper care of her own family.

Furthermore, she was to tell her sister that she should feel grateful that she was in a fine setting where she was well cared for. And, finally, Harriet must tell her sister, firmly and convincingly, that she must become involved in the hospital's recreational program, and that she, Harriet, would see her only once a week from now on. Harriet was understandably reluctant to say all these things to her sister. However, I explained to her how acting out this scene would make it easier for her in the long run. She agreed to do it, and we scheduled our next appointment for two weeks later.

Experience has taught me not to expect miracles. It is a paradox that so many people seek professional help and are so reluctant to change. I was pleased when Harriet appeared at our next meeting, relaxed and smiling. Things were much better with her sister, she reported, but she wasn't going to give me all the credit. She had left my office last time thinking about the imaginary dialogue assignment I had given her, when suddenly it occurred to her,   "My sister is no longer my older sister who can tell me what to do. The roles are reversed now and she needs me to tell her what's best for her." Harriet went on to explain that, through her controlled anger, she was able to gain her sister's attention and respect. "And when I left," Harriet concluded, "my sister told me she loved me and would look forward to seeing me in a week."

Next time you feel angry, try thinking of different, more rewarding ways to deal with the emotion so that it leaves you feeling good about yourself instead of guilty. Think what you would do when a driver approaches you at night and blinds you with his bright lights. You could raise your high beams in retaliation, thus creating two blind drivers on the highway instead of one, or you could merely signal the other driver until the conflict is resolved.

SUMMARY

To summarize these thoughts on anger, remember that no one can make you angry unless you let him or her. Instead of responding on impulse, stand back and determine what actually is happening to you emotionally. Make sure you are not perceiving the situation in a distorted way. Try to understand what underlying expectations, wants, or desires you have that are not being met. Anger usually registers when a person feels that he or she is being treated unfairly. The greater the crime against us, the more angry we feel. Perhaps, listening to the other side of an argument can create a better understanding. For example, I was in a store recently with a friend who tends to be overly defensive about most things. He wanted to buy some lettuce and complained to the clerk that the lettuce was terrible, and that it was a crime to charge so much money for an inferior product. My friend made a few more complaints when the clerk interrupted: "Sir," he began, "you are absolutely correct. If you'll wait just a minute, I can open a fresh crate. I'm sure you'll find a head to your liking."

My friend marveled at the manner in which the clerk handled his complaint, but I wondered why he hadn't avoided the situation in the first place simply by asking the clerk if there were other lettuce heads available. If you get caught up in a situation like that, think of the choices at your disposal. You can accept what you find, you can locate a better source, or you can decide not to buy the item at all. Or you can start an argument. It's not difficult to understand why the expression "hot head" is applied to people with short fuses. They explode too easily and don't take time to think about what's really going on.

Trying to see the other person's point of view, particularly when you are feeling justifiably angry, is never easy. I remember well the day I finished my doctoral dissertation at Columbia University. It was a lengthy piece of research based on three groups of graduate students whom I'd been treating in group therapy all that year. Each session had been carefully analyzed, the charts and statistics were in order, the bibliography was complete, and I fully expected my professor to give me high praise. Instead, he told me that while he enjoyed reading about the successful cases I had presented, he would like to see the same number of unsuccessful cases. My immediate response was anger. Why hadn't he told me that months ago? I asked myself. After I'd collected my thoughts and realized what had to be done, my emotions started to cool down. I knew if I remained angry I'd never complete the assignment. And so I dismissed all the negative feelings and did the extra six months of work. My professor had spoken and I had received his message, loud and clear. The only wise choice I could make was to accept reality and act in my own best interest.

Whatever conflicts you are experiencing in your life, try to settle them without letting them drag on. And don't let relatively minor issues become major ones; save your anger for truly important matters if you must. In the big scheme of things, many annoying incidents are really not even worth becoming angry over. When I drop a jar of coffee in the kitchen I simply clean it up. It serves no purpose to permit that accident to upset me. I save my "angry button" for when it is needed and appropriate, and then I try to use it sparingly. I hope the examples I've offered you in this chapter will motivate you to find more effective ways of dealing with your anger.

Chapter Fifteen

REDUCING STRESS IN YOUR LIFE

It is normal for individuals to react to the physical and emotional stresses of life. What varies greatly from person to person is the amount of stress each one of us experiences as a result of life's daily occurrences and how we react to them. What may be a highly stressful situation to one person may be of little significance to another. But few, if any, of us can avoid the stress that results from such traumatic events as the death of a loved one, the loss of a job, or the onset of a serious illness. On a lower, less serious level, is the stress that comes from such typical experiences as moving from one city to another, starting a new job, making a speech before a large group, or competing in an athletic event. The more confident, self-assured person usually handles these stresses better than the one who struggles through life with a weak self-concept. Often, the latter group will turn to smoking, drinking, or drugs as a way to relieve the stress they feel. Instead of reducing the stress, these actions succeed only in heightening it, because whatever produced the stress in the first place is not dealt with. Sooner or later, stress that is not being addressed will have a damaging effect on one's emotional and physical health.

As a mother, Louise never had much patience with her children. She had always wanted to be an actress, and she resented having to sacrifice her career for the needs of her children. Consequently, everything they did annoyed her. She felt tense and anxious most of the time, and drank and smoked constantly. Still, she denied having any personal problems and refused to get help. Because she did not address what was producing her stress, she developed several common health problems, such as ulcers, colitis, and headaches.

THE PHYSICAL SIDE OF STRESS

A few years ago, I ran in a race in which a fellow competitor suffered a heart attack and died. The incident prompted me to take a stress test. Following the examination, I had an opportunity to speak to the cardiologist at length regarding the subject of stress. He said he was amazed at the poor physical condition of so many of the people he examined. He also commented about the emotional stress people experience, mostly from conflicts in their personal relationships. That kind of stress, he said, can be just as serious as being out of shape physically.

Is stress a factor to be considered in your life? Check the list below to determine how many items apply to you.

1.   **You do not feel relaxed a good part of the time.**

2.   **You are often very irritable or angry.**

3.   **You frequently use alcohol, drugs, or cigarettes to relieve tension.**

4.   **You have a stress-producing problem that is not being attended to.**

5.   **You have difficulty concentrating on everyday events.**

6.   **You feel uncomfortable with people.**

7.   **You have difficulty falling (or staying) asleep.**

8.   **You suffer from nervous habits, such as tics, nail-biting, or stammering.**

If you recognize yourself in the preceding list and you are determined to deal with the normal stresses of everyday living, consider these suggestions that have worked for others in similar situations.

1.   **Take good care of your body.** Everyone needs good food, exercise, and the avoidance of physical abuse. Stop smoking or drinking. Exercise the control you need to treat your body with respect and care. You need your body to live. Do something physical each day to stay in shape, and provide a healthy outlet for the normal tensions that build up in your life: run, walk, play tennis, swim, dance, or get involved in an aerobics program. Put it on your schedule and keep it there. But first, take a stress test so that you'll be sure to do the right kind of exercise for your physical makeup.

2.   Identify other activities that will help you relax. These can be music, art, square-dancing, theater, playing an instrument, sewing, or carpentry. Whatever it is, do it. Find the activities that you enjoy and help you feel calm.

3.   Learn what is producing the stress in your life. Is it a conflict with some person close to you? Have you set an unrealistic goal for yourself, such as becoming financially independent before you're thirty? Examine carefully what intimidates or frustrates you so you can seek solutions to those problems.

4.   Get control of your life. Look over your schedule—are you doing what's best for you? You may be successful on the job, but at what physical and emotional price? Could you be doing the same things with less stress involved? Rearrange your schedule so that you can say to yourself with confidence, "I'm using my time well."

5.   Read. Reading is an excellent way to unwind, to learn, and be mentally stimulated. Many patients have told me they have reduced stress by reading before they go to bed.

6.   Do something nice each day for another person. It is especially gratifying to help people who are not as healthy, strong, capable, or as young as you.

7.   Get a pet. If you have ever had a pet, you know that they can do a lot to help you relax. If you've never owned a pet (and it can be a fish or a bird or any number of possibilities—not just the furry, cuddly ones) you may want to give it a try.

8.   Try to reduce your worrying. Constant worrying is nothing less than programming yourself to be tense. The mind needs to relax, not worry constantly. You have to be concerned about important issues in your life, but that doesn't mean you must always focus in on doom and gloom. Don't sweat the small stuff, and don't worry about something that may never happen!

Think over these suggestions and determine whether any can help you. Stress that goes untreated can become a killer. Ignore it at your risk. If you cannot find relief, talk to your physician. Find out what's causing your problem and take appropriate steps to "get the stress out of your life."

Chapter Sixteen

MAKING SENSE OF RELATIONSHIPS

Jill is the mother of three children with all the trappings of a successful married life. She and her husband, Don, enjoy good health, own a nice home in the suburbs, and their children seem happy. Jill has been successful in real estate sales. Socially, she and Don have plenty of friends, and they manage to go on vacation every year. "I have no big complaints," Jill insists. "Don and I have been married fourteen years and we like each other a lot. Many of our friends are experiencing sexual problems, but I can't complain about that. We have sex often enough, and we both enjoy it. After saying all that, you probably think I'm crazy, but the truth is, I want more. If Don and I weren't sleeping together, I wonder: Would we really need each other?"

Clearly, Jill felt something was missing in their relationship. She described her husband as a gregarious fellow who seemed to get along with everyone. He was also a terrific father, who coached his son's little league baseball team and was always there when he was needed.

"Doesn't it all sound too good to be true?" Jill asked. "We don't even have any money problems, and I really enjoy selling real estate. I enjoy the children, too. It almost makes me feel guilty being here."

With that, Jill began to cry. After a few moments, I said, "You have been telling me mostly good things about your family. I wonder why you are crying and what really brought you here for help." This is what Jill told me: "I've thought about my unhappiness many times, but I always felt so guilty about feeling so dissatisfied. On the surface, Don and I have so much going for us. Perhaps the trouble began when I got pregnant before we were married. It didn't seem to be any big tragedy at the time, although I never expected the negative reaction I got from my mother. She made me feel like the worst person alive, and she has never let me forget what happened. She made such a big issue out of it that it put a damper on the marriage right from the start. It made me wonder later on if I had been forced into the marriage. It wasn't the way I wanted to start out, that's for sure. Over the years, I've come to understand my problems with my mother, but I'm convinced our marriage isn't what it could be. During the early years, I was busy taking care of the children while Don was finishing college. Then most of his energy was geared toward starting his own business. Our conversations centered around where we were going on vacation, what things we were going to buy, who we should invite for dinner, and Don's business. But, somehow, we never seemed to make each other feel good. We talked about events, not feelings. When the kids became less dependent on me, I discovered that work outside the home was satisfying and very stimulating. I was able to use my mind for something other than child-rearing and household chores. In fact, I was finding more excitement on the job than when I was with Don. We weren't spending much time together, either, and we had only a vague idea what the other was thinking, feeling, or doing. If we ever did care, that curiosity faded away long ago. Now we both go almost automatically on our own, independent ways. I've noticed we show a lot more interest and enthusiasm when we're talking to other people than we do with each other. But whenever I start thinking about how careless we're getting in our marriage, I say to myself, 'Jill, you're just looking for trouble where it doesn't exist.' I began to notice that I wasn't rushing around doing things for Don anymore, like making his favorite meals, for example. He, in turn, would promise to fix something for months and then instead spend a whole day helping our next door neighbor. Another thing I've noticed: we have no difficulty staying awake when we're at a party, but we both fall asleep in front of the television set every night when we're alone. Sometimes, we act as if the other one isn't even there!"

Jill must have been storing those thoughts for a long time.

"I don't know when it happened," she continued, "but I have begun talking to myself, asking a lot of nagging questions about our relationship. One question that keeps popping into my head is, 'Why aren't we talking to each other?' We did at one time, or did we? You reach the point where you don't really remember. I also noticed a growing impatience in Don. It was like a kind of low tolerance for me and what I had to say. At times, he is quick to anger, cutting me off with silence for a few days. I know he is upset with me for some reason, but I can't get him to talk about it. I feel like I did when I was a child and my mother wouldn't speak to me. It makes me feel really bad and frustrated, because this whole thing is hard to understand, much less talk to Don about. I know I'm painting a picture of doom and gloom, but I'm only telling you what I feel is happening more and more. Maybe Don will give you a whole different story. Lately, I've been expecting him to get angry, so I've held back from saying what's on my mind. I think he's censoring what he says to me, too. One of his pet complaints is that I make too big a deal out of these issues. I don't even know what he means by that."

I listened to Jill until she stopped. She told me she had told me the whole story, but, for some reason, I felt there was more that she had not told me. "Why do I get the feeling there is something else?" I asked.

"I wasn't sure I should tell you," she confessed, "but I really want our marriage to work. If I'm not honest with you, I know everything could be lost. The truth is, I've been seeing another man."

Jill's story came as no surprise to me, for infidelity is a common ingredient these days among relationships that have lost whatever understanding, acceptance, compassion, and open communication they may have had in the beginning. After a number of sessions with both of them, Jill and Don decided to place a priority on resolving their marital difficulties, at which they were thankfully successful. So many couples are not willing to face the fact that they need help, however. Others have found the courage to seek help, but have not had what it takes to work out a resolution the way Jill and Don did. Often, when it's obvious that a relationship is in trouble, the couple involved will leave my office saying, "We decided we can work it out on our own," or, "We talked it over and we aren't angry with each other anymore," or, "You've been a big help, and we understand what to do now." In most cases, it was obvious to me that these people were bound to continue doing the same unhealthy things to their relationships.

I had the honor of speaking to the graduating class at Colby College some years ago. The title of my talk was *Beyond College*. I spoke about the importance of thinking and doing what is healthy. I told the bright-eyed group that they were intelligent and should employ sound judgment. One of the examples I used was directing them to remove themselves from any relationships that were not meaningful. The next day I was walking around the campus when a young lady approached me. She said she had been in a relationship for some time that was indeed not healthy. The young man she had been dating was abusive and selfish. She said she had hoped he would change, but was pessimistic about that happening. She did not know why it took her so long to realize she had to terminate the relationship, but she wanted me to know she finally did. "I guess I had to hear your speech yesterday to get the motivation to act," she said.

If you feel your relationship or marriage is not what you want it to be, start now to change whatever you sense isn't working. The first step is to examine your own role in the relationship. You can't improve a two-person relationship without understanding yourself first.

Look at yourself by asking the following questions. If you are having trouble in some of the following areas, then it may not be your relationship that is not working—it could be that you need to help yourself first. Once you address your own personal situation, you will often find that your relationship improves tremendously as you are able to offer yourself as an emotionally strong, stable partner.

- Are there any experiences still affecting you from your childhood?

- On a scale of one to ten, rate yourself on self-confidence. If you scored less than seven, you should determine what is preventing you from viewing yourself in a positive way.

- Are you experiencing any major problems in the primary areas of your life, such as having difficulty interacting with people, or a conflict on the job?

- How are you doing with the important people in your life? If conflicts exist, are you able to come up with good resolutions?

- When conflicts arise, can you meet the problems head-on? Or do you make excuses, deny the problems exist, blame others for them, or run away?

- What kinds of emotions dominate your life? If strong negative feelings are occurring frequently, they probably indicate some unresolved conflicts need to be tended to.

- Is your body sending out messages worth listening to? Stomachaches, headaches, insomnia, eating problems, all can be important warning signals. Have your physician rule out any organic reasons for your ailments.

- Where are your thoughts most often directed? Is your mind relatively at peace with the world, or do you spend a lot of time worrying? Do you daydream to the extent of not being able to concentrate properly?

- How well are you taking care of yourself? Do you drink too much, take drugs, or abuse yourself in other ways?

If the answers to these questions lead you to believe that you have some work to do personally, then you should address your issues for yourself before looking to fix a relationship. On the other hand, if you find that the answers to these questions imply that you are relatively stable, then there are many things you can do to improve your relationship.

Among the hundreds of couples I've tried to steer toward a more meaningful relationship, a great many, unfortunately, refused to let me help them. Instead, they offered a multitude of excuses for why they must continue their safe, comfortable, and conflictual relationships. They ran from help because their inner defenses would not allow an open, honest analysis of their marriages.

To all those people who want to grow and create better relationships; to all those people who feel their relationships are not measuring up to their expectations; to all those people who seek information about how to deal with marital conflicts; to all those people who want to enjoy sex and not avoid intimacy; to all of you people, I offer these tested prescriptions for stimulating, supportive, and meaningful relationships:

- Take a good, hard look at yourself and ask: Am I putting my best foot forward? Am I doing all I can to make myself an alive, attractive, and appealing person? Stay in shape and look your best for yourself as well as for your chosen partner.

- Try to understand and resolve any problems that cause you to behave negatively in a relationship. Be honest, not defensive, in your assessment. None of us is perfect. In your self-analysis, be sure to include your relationship with your parents.

- Try to please your mate more. Learn what makes him or her happy, then do what you can to satisfy those needs. By so doing, you'll be saying, "I care."

- Be ready to listen to your partner. Don't be too quick to criticize, interrupt, or lose interest. If the message you're getting is unclear, ask what it means until you understand.

- Don't be accusatory, disrespectful, or derisive toward your partner. Finding fault with someone almost always produces anger and retaliation. Try a little compassion, understanding, and support instead.

- Make more time available for intimacy. Discuss sex openly so that you can both understand what pleases each other. If you have worked out the other parts of your relationship, sex can be beautiful.

- Become more knowledgeable about sex and marriage by reading books and articles on the subjects. Discover new ways to keep your relationship alive and well.

- Communicate with each other more effectively. Make your thoughts and feelings known to each other. This may seem difficult to do at first, especially if you have been guarded and evasive in your interaction. But not saying what you really think and feel can result only in misunderstandings and mis-interpretations.

- Be a strong, independent person and carry your end of the load in the relationship. With independence comes self-respect. Do not expect your mate to do for you what you can do for yourself. Don't be like a child who must be cared for; act like a mature adult.

- Express your appreciation for each other. Too many people take their mates for granted. If your partner pleases you, acknowledge it.

- Ask your partner's opinions about matters that are important to you. If you don't ask, you will never know. By asking, you are also sending the message, "I value what you have to say."

- Treat each other with the same courtesy and attention you show to friends and acquaintances. Too often, we take our long-time partners for granted and treat them dismissively, especially compared to the way we treat complete strangers. Showing interest and attention to your spouse or partner can have an immediately strong effect on the way he or she feels about you and your relationship.

- Respect yourself and each other in words as well as actions. But do not be afraid to argue. Arguments based on honest differences of opinion sometimes pave the way to better understanding.

- Finally, love does not mean sacrificing one's individuality or integrity; it is an expression of affection and respect. Marriage is a shared relationship in which both partners are accepted for their own strengths and weaknesses, and the stronger both partners are individually (emotionally and mentally), the stronger and more fulfilling the relationship will be.

Chapter Seventeen

WHEN TO SEEK
PROFESSIONAL HELP

I truly believe that individuals have the capacity to resolve their own personal problems. Most of this book has been designed to help you recognize how you can best help yourself. Given the intellect, motivation and will, there is little the average person cannot accomplish on his or her own. Never underestimate anyone's ability to deal with serious problems, to build a relationship, or resolve a conflict. Even if you do not have all the answers, you can still turn to family members, close friends, teachers, the clergy, or someone special whom you can trust to help sort things out. When all else fails, there are many professionals who are trained to understand and solve personal problems and whose counsel you can seek.

When is the appropriate time to seek professional help, and to whom should you turn? Here are a few considerations in determining the need for professional help:

1. How extensive is your problem? Severe, moderate, or mild?

2. How effective have you been in the past in resolving your difficulties?

3. Is your problem a temporary and situational reaction to a specific trauma?

4. How deeply are your problems interfering with important areas, such as your opinion of yourself, your relationships with other people, your productivity, your sense of fulfillment, and so forth?

5. Do you find yourself using many defense mechanisms (e.g., avoidance, denial, blame)?

6.   Is your thinking clear or cloudy? How is your ability to make judgments? Have your current problems made it more difficult for you to think clearly?

7.   To what extent do you consider your present behavior peculiar?

8.   Do you have the mental and emotional capacity to cope with the issues at hand?

9.   To what extent do you exhibit helplessness and hopelessness?

10.   Are you in danger of harming yourself or others? Do you have suicidal and/ or homicidal thoughts, intentions, or actions? Do you engage in any self-destructive behaviors?

Professional help is strongly recommended if you are feeling less able to cope with your life's circumstances and you have answered the questions above in a way that tells you that your mental and/or physical health is in danger. You may have noticed that the questions get more severe as you read down the list, so if you have trouble with your answers toward the end of the list, that is more of an issue and more of a reason to seek professional help than if you had issues with the questions toward the top of the list. Additionally, if you had a hard time understanding how to answer the questions, then again, it may be wise to sit down with a trained professional and get an objective opinion as to the severity of your present condition. If doubts remain, you can always seek out a second or third opinion.

You cannot avoid or deny the existence of problems that are interfering with your life. If you are not happy, relaxed, and at peace, there is a problem to be resolved. If you do not see yourself able to make progress on your own, then seek out assistance from one of the many professionals who are trained to help you. You should not have to wait until you are suicidal in order to seek help. Each state has licensed psychologists, psychiatrists, and social workers to whom you can turn. Many states have license requirements for marriage counselors. Hospitals, university counseling centers, and mental health clinics are usually supervised and staffed by competent trained personnel or graduate students in training. Some clergymen are trained counselors too. The county or state medical and psychological associations, or the state or national associations of psychiatric social workers are other good sources of information. Most professional groups publish directories listing names and addresses, which can be found in your local library or by calling the executive secretary of any given association.

Unfortunately, the number of professionals working in the field who are poorly trained is alarmingly high. I urge you to check the credentials of any professional person or group with whom you plan to discuss these matters. The mere fact that a professional person is licensed and has the proper credentials does not tell you everything you need to know, of course, about that individual's reputation, training, or compatibility. Such information can be acquired, at least in part, by making inquiries at the professional association office, or by discussing the matter with a professional practitioner whom you trust—your doctor or dentist, for examples. The question of selecting a therapist whose frame of reference is rational-emotive, cognitive, interpersonal relations, psychoanalytic, or behavioral is not really critical. If you have found a trained person with whom you feel comfortable, you are well on your way to getting the assistance you need. Feel free at the first instance to discuss any issue, including the cost and duration of therapy. Any good therapist should be more than willing to discuss whatever is on your mind. If you are hesitant about seeking help, you will probably feel much relieved once you're in the therapist's office. If not, either you are resisting help or are not responding to the therapist, or the therapist may not be the best one for you.

Once you've made your decision, enter the therapy program with an open mind. Give it a fair chance. Realize that your problem didn't develop overnight and cannot disappear magically in a few therapy sessions. Your therapist, after all, could be very important in helping you sort out some distorted thinking and behavior on your part. Think of it as one of the most important investments in time and money you can make (you are talking about happiness, peace of mind), so be prepared to spend the time and money necessary. Many people carry insurance to help with the payment for such services. There are also low-cost facilities available that are subsidized by state and county governments.

How effective is modern psychotherapy? It depends largely on the patient's motivation and commitment to change. Many people do not want to deal directly and effectively with their problems. They wait until there is a crisis before they call for expert help. They wait until the marriage is all but ruined, or a child runs away, or severe depression has rendered them unable to work. Medication can help in some cases, but it is not a substitute for what transpires between therapist and patient. It requires great effort on the parts of both patient and therapist. It does not involve symptom relief only, but more the gaining of control over your thinking and behavior, so that you may treat yourself in a respectful manner. In short, psychotherapy means replacing negative attitudes—the ones that have caused you so much misery—with healthy, positive thoughts. If you have tried, but have been unable to help yourself by reading and practicing what is in this book, then you should really seek professional help. Your life, your personal peace, depends on it.

PART FIVE

EMERGING STRONGER

Chapter Eighteen

YOUR NEW ABILITIES

I hope you have had a meaningful experience reading *Secrets from the Sofa*, and that it has enriched your life. It was my intention to give you a specific plan to attack issues and to elicit your commitment to make the necessary changes in your life.

You have been given ample evidence to show that thoughts, perceptions, and attitudes affect feelings. You are now aware of the importance of striving for the best possible feelings—those enabling you to relax and feel proud. It is terrific to think positively about life and boast of increased self-esteem.

As you have attended carefully and completed the exercises in the book, you should have greater skill recognizing thoughts and behaviors that are not in your best interest. Also, you will be able to make more sense of your early years as they relate to who you are as a person. You have learned that childhood matters, but, in the case of childhood misfortunes, anything learned can be unlearned. We are always capable of regrouping. When you listen to your parental tapes, hear what has made you feel a sense of worth and disregard what was inadvertently hampering.

Acknowledge newly discovered strengths and know that you have unlimited resources to cope. Be aware that, in most instances, you can depend upon yourself like no other person for whatever decisions confront you.

Your new perceptions emphasize that you no longer have to tolerate what is not satisfying, be it a joke, relationships, or anything else. You now have greater power to control your life. If negative thoughts crop up, you know that they have a source to be uncovered.

I hope too that you have learned that significant change takes time and that you have the patience to wait to achieve your goals.

You have been introduced to various coping styles of thought patterns and behaviors utilized to avoid change. The typical defense mechanisms employed by individuals also have been presented to you. You have learned that it is unwise to stay with what is safe and comfortable if it means not living up to your potential.

You now know to expect anxiety, denial, and resistance when venturing into unexplored territory. But you also know that these are not generally effective ways to deal with problems.

It is natural that we all have dreams of what we would like our life to be, changes we would like to make. By now, you know change requires courage, confidence, and self-assurance. You have been encouraged to make change happen and not wait until confronted with a crisis.

You understand that it is important to acknowledge your strengths. Every time you attempt to be stronger makes you stronger even if your effort is not a hundred percent successful.

You have had an opportunity to discover your unique self with all your qualities. No longer do you need to be held back by fears. They can be your signal to be challenged and stronger. You will hopefully no longer waste your time with behaviors that do not make you feel self-respect and proud. You have seen how to set the scene for becoming a more interesting, productive, relaxed, confident, and self-reliant person.

You understand that you need not be overwhelmed by your problems because you know how to seek solutions by facing them more directly. You should no longer permit yourself to be abused by your own negative thoughts and bad habits that can overcome your life, ruin your health, or be life threatening. Every change you can make for the better will offer an opportunity for you to become stronger and happier. If you now perceive yourself as a stronger, more worthwhile person, you deserve to be complimented.

I believe people generally are a good deal stronger than they give themselves credit for being. Reading is an excellent way to discover one's strengths. That is why this book came to be. The many suggestions and examples were designed to stimulate the readers to actually be their own psychologist. Therefore, a great portion of the book was developed to help you recognize how you could help yourself. I will repeat this thought: Never underestimate your ability to cope with the most intricate problems. Set your sights for what you wish to achieve, be it a better relationship or resolving a conflict.

One of my hobbies is the restoration of antique furniture. Often I can take a battered piece badly in need of repair and transform it into a work of beauty. It doesn't happen magically. The task requires a lot of patience and labor. But the end product usually results in a magnificent piece of furniture being produced.

Trying to help individuals enhance the quality of their lives is quite different from restoring furniture. The furniture usually responds to my loving care. People are prone to stay with what seems comfortable and secure. For those reasons, there is a natural resistance to change. It was my intention in writing *Secrets from the Sofa* to enable the reader to escape from the excuses and defenses that hold them back from living the best life possible. Having studied human behavior for many years, it has always been my dream to have a positive effect on a larger population than one psychotherapist can see in an office. To be afforded the opportunity to make your life and the lives of other readers better is indeed gratifying.

People acknowledge that the brevity of life is astounding, but many do not treat their days, months, and years as precious. It is a gift to be alive with whatever condition one is in. Treat life as the valuable gift it is.

You may have surprised yourself with the progress made since reading this book. You may even wonder if the changes will be permanent. I can tell you emphatically that whatever growth you have been able to achieve can be permanent. All you have to do is continue to practice your newfound ways of coping, continue to think positively about yourself, and stay focused on your goals toward your personal peace process.

I want to wish you the best life possible. Think and act with all the strength you can generate. May you find new and exciting rewards with your newfound information, insights, and tools for change.

ADDITIONAL RESOURCES

National Organizations
National Mental Health Association (NMHA)
1021 Prince Street
Alexandria, Virginia 22314-2971
Main (703) 684-7722
Toll free (800) 433-5959
Fax (703) 684-5968
Web http://www.nmha.org

American Psychiatric Association
1400 K Street, NW
Suite 501
Washington, DC 20005
Toll free (888) 852-8330
Web http://www.psych.org

American Psychological Association
750 First Street, NE
Washington, DC 20002-4242
Toll free (800) 964-2000
Web http://www.apa.org

National Alliance for the Mentally Ill
200 N. Glebe Rd.
Suite 1015
Arlington, Virginia 22203
Toll free (800) 950-NAMI
Web http://www.nami.org

National Depressive and Manic Depressive Association
730 N. Franklin Street
Chicago, IL 60610
Toll free (800) 82-NDMDA
Web http://www.ndmda.org

National Institute of Mental Health
6100 Executive Building
Rm. 8184, MSC 9663
Bethesda, Maryland 20892
Main (301) 443-4211
Toll free (800) 421-4211
Web http://www.nimh.nih.gov

National Foundation for Depressive Illnesses, Inc.
PO Box 257
New York, New York 10116
Toll free (800) 239-1265
Web http://www.depression.org

National Mental Illness Screening Project
One Washington Street
Suite 304
Wellesley, MA 02181-1706
Main (781) 239-0071
Toll free (800) 573-4433
Web http://www.nmisp.org

American Association of Marital and Family Therapy
1133 15th Street, NW Suite 300
Washington, DC 20005-2710
(202) 452-0109
Web http://www.aamft.org

Obsessive-Compulsive Foundation, Inc.
337 Notch Hill Road
North Branford, CT 06471
(203) 315-2190
Web http://www.info@ocfoundation.org

The American Psychological Society
1010 Vermont Avenue, NW Suite 1100
Washington, DC 20005-4907
(202) 783-2077
Web http://www.psychologicalscience.org

**Web sites to use and important online mental health resources
(The following are general information sites related to psychology and mental health):**

Links to specific areas of mental illness and psychological issues:
http://www.cyber-psych.com

An encyclopedia of mental health illnesses, medications, treatment, and research findings:
http://www.mentalhealth.com

An online information service for psychological professionals and clients:
http://www.onlinepsych.com

Access to detailed services available for mental and medical health problems:
http://www.realtime.net/~mmjw

Provides access to mental health information:
http://www.sover.net/~schwcof/links.html

A service for people to enhance their lives through psychology:
http://www.psychology.com

Psychology resource and search engine:
http://www.cyber-psych.com/resource.html

Psychology journals:
http://www.cyber-psych.com/journal.html

National Mental Health Organizations:
http://www.cyber-psych.com/national.html

The American Academy of Experts in Traumatic Stress
http://www.aaets.org

National Directory of Psychologists (lists licensed psychologists by state)
http://www.psychologyinfo.com/directory

The following are specific topics within psychology and mental health (each individual site listed here provides many links to other related sites):

Addictions:
http://www.cyber-psych.com/addict.html

Anxiety Disorders:
http://www.cyber-psych.com/anxiety.html

Child Abuse:
http://www.cyber-psych.com/trauma.html http://www/kidspeace.org A center for children in crisis

Child and Parenting Issues:
http://www.cyber-psych.com/childhood.html

Domestic Abuse:
http://www.cyber-psych.com/domestic.html

Eating Disorders:
http://www.cyber-psych.com/eat.html

Employee Assistance:
http://www.cyber-psych.com/eap.html

Grief and Loss:
http://www.cyber-psych.com/grief.html

Incest Survivors Resource Network International:
http://www.zianet.com/isrni

Mood Disorders:
http://www.cyber-psych.com/mood.html

Self-Help/Support Groups:
http://www.cyber-psych.com/self.html

Self-Injury:
http://www.cyber-psych.com/selfinjury.html

Sexual Abuse Recovery:
http://www.cyber-psych.com/sexabuse.html

Sex Information:
http://www.cyber-psych.com/sex.html

Sleep Disorders and Dreams:
http://www.cyber-psych.com/sleep.html

Social Work:
http://www.cyber-psych.com/social.html

Trauma and Recovery:
http://www.cyber-psych.com/trauma.html

978-0-595-41432-1
0-595-41432-X